Teach® Yourself

Motivating People

Sue Stockdale and Clive Steeper

www.inaweek.co.uk

First published in Great Britain in 2014 by Hodder & Stoughton. An Hachette UK company.

First published in US in 2014 by The McGraw-Hill Companies, Inc.

Also available in ebook

In A

Sue Stockdale and Clive Steeper

The Teach Yourself series has been trusted around the world for over 60 years. This series of 'In a Week' business books is designed to help people at all levels to further their careers. Learn in a week what the experts learn in a lifetime.

Sue Stock▮▮▮▮▮▮▮▮▮▮▮▮▮▮▮▮aker, executive coach and
leadership specialist. ▮▮▮▮▮▮ith leaders and teams in
some of Europe's top companies, helping them to achieve
exceptional performance. As a highly motivated individual, Sue
has represented Scotland in athletics and was the first British
woman to ski to the North Pole. Her advice on motivation and
business regularly appears in the media. www.suestockdale.com

Clive Steeper has been a business leader running high-growth
companies for over 25 years including roles as Managing
Director in the UK, USA and Asia. Central to Clive's success
has been his ability to motivate people and teams to achieve
more than they imagined possible. He now works as an
executive coach, consultant and facilitator. In his spare time
Clive is a keen motorsports competitor and instructor.
www.clivesteeper.com

*We dedicate this book to those people who have given
us the impetus to face and overcome life's challenges.*

Contents

Introduction

What's going to make this week different from any other? It's the beginning of another week. Think about what challenges you may be facing. How motivated are you? How motivated are those with whom you work? You could be the difference in making this a better week for yourself and others. With the help of this book, you can spend this week looking at how you can improve your own motivation and the motivation of others.

This book will explore motivation from a number of perspectives, including motivation needs, explored in the work of Abraham Maslow and Frederick Herzberg, and motivation drivers, explored in the work of Harry Harlow and Edward Deci.

Traditional thinking around the subject has been that, after satisfying our basic human needs of hunger, thirst and copulation, our primary motivation for behaving in a particular way is based on the rewards or punishment we receive. This can be regarded as **external motivation**.

Over the last century, pioneering work has helped us to recognize the significance of **intrinsic motivation** and the motivation we obtain from the **performance of the task**. Research has shown that we take pleasure (motivational drive) from solving puzzles. Work conducted by Deci in the late 1960s and early 1970s discovered that external rewards (e.g. money) can in some situations create only a short-term gain, and that longer-term motivation and drive come from within. This is now known as **Self-Determination Theory** (SDT) and it deals with people's essential psychological needs and deep-rooted development preferences.

In motivating others, it is a real advantage to have a sound understanding of an individual's level of self-motivation and self-determination. This means gaining an appreciation of the behaviours and motivators behind the choices that people make without any external influence and interference. This insight can help to inform you on how to motivate them.

Even in this short introduction we can begin to see that, while motivating others can be complex, there are some fundamental aspects that, if followed, will help you to do this effectively.

Sue Stockdale and Clive Steeper

SUNDAY

What's in it for me?

Some people are naturally good at motivating others, but for most people it is a leadership skill that they learn. A common mistake is to assume that other people are motivated by the same things you are, so you use that approach with them. Sadly, that rarely works – as a manager you need to view each person as an individual and learn to listen to the language they use, and observe how they behave, in order to work out a personalized strategy for them. That might sound like hard work, particularly if you have a large number of people to manage, but it pays off in the long term, when you develop a highly motivated team.

If you are prepared to embark on the journey of learning how to motivate others, first you have be motivated yourself. Think about what makes you excited and energized at work. Often, when you are motivated and enthusiastic about something, it is easier to bring others along with you. They get caught up in your excitement, which can be contagious.

In today's chapter you will be able to reflect on what motivates you, so that you can generate energy and passion for the activities that get you fired up. It will also explain some of the best-known models and theories developed by experts, including Maslow, McClelland and Herzberg, that help us understand more about how people behave and are motivated.

Understanding your motive for action

Motivation = motive for action

What's your motive for action?

Any person becomes motivated when they want to do something. This drive, which comes from inside them, causes them to take action. It's their motive. However, this is not the same as being incentivized to take action, which often brings some type of external reward.

> ## Case study: inner motivation
>
> Take the story of George, who had recently been promoted to manager in a large organization. He felt that it was important to get to know his team, so he took time to have coffee with them and learn more about each member. George was motivated to find out what made them tick because he would then be able to manage them better. George's manager also noticed his efforts and later commented that George had fitted into the team really easily and there was a very positive atmosphere. In summary:
>
> **Motive for action** = To be able to manage team effectively.
>
> **Behaviour** = He took time to have coffee with each person.
>
> **Result** = He built rapport and trust with each team member.
>
> **Additional benefit** = Manager recognized George's efforts.

So it is useful to become more aware of what motivates you to take action. Use the questions below to reflect on this statement. Think of a time at work when you were highly motivated.

- What was going on?
- Who was involved?
- How did you feel?

- What caused it to be motivating for you?
- What did you do?

Then repeat the above exercise for a time when you were really demotivated and lacking energy for work. Analyse both sets of answers, thinking about the specific factors that caused you to behave in different ways.

Now list any insights you have gained that could help you be more motivated and also how you could avoid becoming demotivated.

> **'We cannot change anything until we accept it. Condemnation does not liberate; it oppresses.'**
> Carl Jung

Knowing yourself

It is important to be aware of how you are motivated, particularly if you are a manager, because other people will look to you for inspiration – it will be that much harder to encourage other people if you are not motivated yourself.

Think about what motivates you. For some people, it may seem obvious: money is the main motivator at work. While many of us might agree with this view, the research proves otherwise. Surveys and research studies repeatedly show that other factors motivate more than money. For example, a survey published in UK newspaper *The Times* in 2004 showed that the main reasons people leave their jobs were lack of stimulus and no opportunity for advancement.

The notion that long-term motivation really comes from within is important to remember as a manager. Many people fall into the trap of thinking that a salary increase will motivate someone to perform better. It may do in the short term, but over a longer period of time other factors (intrinsic motivators) are also needed.

Motivation must come from within.

To help you learn about motivation, there are some well-known theories and models that are useful to learn about. They will help you understand what's really going inside other people's minds and how this causes them to behave as they do. This then helps you to unlock their potential and work out how to approach each person in ways that will yield positive results.

Herzberg's theory of motivation

Frederick Herzberg's theory of motivation is one of the best-known pieces of research in the field. In 1959 he, together with Bernard Mausner and Barbara Bloch Snyderman, published *The Motivation to Work*, which showed that in general people will be initially motivated to achieve **extrinsic needs** ('hygiene' factors) at work because they are unhappy without them. Examples include good salary, working conditions and interpersonal relationships. Once these needs are satisfied, however, the effect soon wears off – that is, job satisfaction is temporary.

People are only truly motivated when they satisfy the needs that Herzberg identified as **intrinsic needs** ('motivators'), such as achievement, advancement and personal development, which represent a far deeper level of meaning and fulfilment.

Herzberg's theory of motivation

Extrinsic needs (hygiene factors)	Intrinsic needs (notivators)
Company policy	Achievement
Supervision	Recognition
Salary	Work itself
Interpersonal relations	Responsibility
Physical working conditions	Advancement

> Think about how Herzberg's theory applies to you.
> What gives you the greatest satisfaction at work?

If you were given a choice – you could either take a rewarding job where you had a high degree of personal control over your work, and a salary double what you are earning, or you could have a job on a production line where you performed fairly repetitive tasks with little control over your work, in poor working conditions and limited promotion opportunities and received a salary three times what you are earning – which would you choose for the long term?

Meta Programs – noticing how language motivates you

Another concept that influences our motivation is Meta Programs. These mental processes enable us to filter the mass of information that we take in each day, and to decide on which bits we should pay attention to.

Meta Programs were identified in the 1970s by researchers Richard Bandler and Leslie Cameron-Bandler, and the initial set of Meta Program patterns were then described by Leslie Cameron-Bandler in collaboration with David Gordon, Robert Dilts and Maribeth Meyers-Anderson.

To work out what your filters are, you need to pay attention to the language you use. For example, one person may be motivated by losing weight whereas another may be encouraged by becoming healthier. Both are different ways to describe a similar outcome, and will motivate people according

SUNDAY

MONDAY

TUESDAY

WEDNESDAY

THURSDAY

FRIDAY

SATURDAY

to their Meta Programs. If you use the wrong one to encourage a colleague, you may quickly realize whether it works or not according to their reaction, because they will literally 'filter out' what you are saying. In this example, one is focused on getting away from the problem (being overweight) and avoiding loss and the other is focused on going towards the solution (feeling healthier) and gaining something.

These Meta Programs manage, guide and direct other mental processes and influence how we are motivated. Each one is on a continuum, with the opposite preferences described below being at either end of the spectrum. Both are equally valid, so there is no bad or good preference.

Away from – Towards

People with a 'Towards' preference are motivated by future goals and the enjoyment they get from achieving them. Their language will be future oriented – for example, 'When I achieve this goal I will feel great.'

Those with an 'Away From' preference are focused on avoiding pain or problems, and they talk about what they don't want to happen. Their language will include words and phrases like 'reduce', 'avoid', 'minimize' and 'get away from'.

In business, you might think that most successful people would have a 'Towards' rather than 'away from' focus – after all, in marketing literature we tend to read phrases like 'make a million', 'achieve your ideal future', 'get your dream job'. However, that is not always the case.

The Scottish golfer Colin Montgomerie acknowledges that he was driven as much by the fear of losing as by achieving a win. This also links with the theory of Loss Aversion developed by Daniel Kahneman and Amos Tversky (1984), which highlights people's tendency to strongly prefer avoiding losses to acquiring gains.

Reactive – Proactive

'Proactive' people will put their hand up first to take on a job without having all the parts of the job clearly defined because they just like to get started. People who are 'Reactive' prefer to wait and see what others do first, because they want to reflect and think about what to do before doing it.

Internal – External

People with an 'Internal' preference know inside how they are doing. They don't need to have any recognition from others to feel validated.

Those with an 'External' preference need others to tell them how they are doing. They will want to seek feedback from other people to confirm that they are on the right track.

Options – Procedures

People who have an 'Options' preference will rarely make a quick decision without looking at all the options available. Those with a 'Procedures' focus, by contrast, will expect that there is a 'right way' to achieve a task and like the reassurance of following a tried-and-tested method.

Global – Specific

Those with a 'Global' preference like getting an overview or summary as they like to see the big picture, but may appear vague or provide a lack of detail. Those who prefer 'Specific' enjoy the detail and want others to have all the information that they believe is important.

Sameness – Difference

People with a 'Sameness' preference enjoy things remaining constant and, if they get a new task, want to know how it's similar to something they are already familiar with.

Those with a 'Difference' preference enjoy change and are motivated by things being new and unfamiliar.

If you think about each pair of preferences and work out which ones you prefer, you will be more aware of how Meta Programs influence your own motivation. Then consider in turn each person that you have to motivate, and notice the language they use so that you can work out which preferences they have, and what words are likely to be more effective when you communicate with them.

Summary of the Meta Programs

Key patterns	How they affect people's motivation
Away From – Towards	Towards – will want to know about rewards, future achievements, goals Away From – you will need to explain how the task will avoid pain, problems, outcomes they don't want
Reactive – Proactive	Proactive – like to be told 'go for it' or just do it! Reactive – prefer to be given direction on a task before they get started
External – Internal	Internal – prefer to make their own internal decisions and have no need to get confirmation from others (e.g. a regular review is less important) External – like to refer to the external advice of others (e.g. a regular review will be important as they want to know that they are doing a good job)
Procedures – Options	Options – will enjoy having a variety of options to consider and may feel threatened by lack of choice Procedures – they like processes and knowing the 'right way' of carrying out a task
Specific – Global	Global – like to be presented with the key points or overview and don't mind things being vague Specific – prefer having the precise detail and factual information
Difference – Sameness	Sameness – look for things that match what they already know and want their world to remain the same Difference – notice what's different and prefer change to be constant

Maslow's Hierarchy of Needs

Another model that can help you to work out what drives you is Maslow's Hierarchy of Needs. This is a well-known tool and is likely one that you will refer to time and time again in the future. What it helps you to do is work out what the underlying needs are of those you interact with, including your boss!

For example, when a new employee joins a team their initial behaviour is often driven by the need to feel that they are part of the team. Once they have been accepted, their needs change and they have a greater need to be recognized and have a level of status within the team. However, if the situation at work changed and there was a high degree of uncertainty about even having a job, their need would then be focused on feeling safe and secure.

If you are able to work out what a person's needs are at any given time, you will find it far easier to come up with ways to help address those needs. Abraham Maslow, a professor of psychology, recognized that humans have these differing needs and so he created a hierarchy that explained the sequence in which these needs are satisfied.

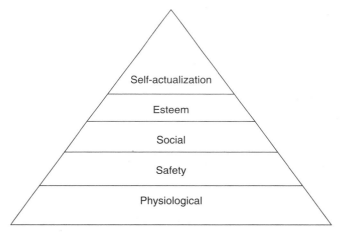

Maslow's Hierarchy of Needs

Physiological needs

Maslow believed that the most basic needs we have are those that are vital to survival – for example water, food, air and sleep. These are the most instinctive needs in the hierarchy and all other needs become secondary until these physiological needs are met.

Safety needs

These include the need for physical safety and security. Security needs are important for survival, but they are not as demanding as physiological needs. Examples of security needs include a desire for steady employment, safe neighbourhoods and shelter from the environment.

Social needs

These include the need to belong and for love and affection. Relationships – whether friendships, romantic attachments or family ties – help fulfil this need for companionship and acceptance, as does involvement in social, community or work groups.

Esteem needs

After the first three needs in the hierarchy have been satisfied, esteem needs become increasingly important. These include the need for things that foster self-esteem, personal worth, social recognition and accomplishment. At work, this can be symbolized by the type of car you drive or the recognition you get from your manager or peers.

Self-actualization

This is the highest level of Maslow's Hierarchy of Needs. Self-actualizing people are self-aware, concerned with personal growth, less concerned with the opinions of others and interested in fulfilling their potential.

The final two levels (esteem needs and self-actualization) are similar to the intrinsic motivators that Herzberg identified in his theory that was outlined earlier, which confirms that humans are ultimately driven to satisfy their need for achievement, recognition and personal fulfilment.

How to apply Maslow's theory to motivate others

The basis of Maslow's theory is that human beings are motivated by unsatisfied needs, and that the lower levels of needs must be satisfied before higher needs. Here are some examples of this:

● You cannot motivate someone to achieve their sales target (Esteem) when they're having problems with their marriage (Social).

- You cannot expect someone to work effectively as a team member (Social) when they believe their job security is threatened (Safety).

Case study: using Maslow's Hierarchy of Needs

Take the experience of Suzie. She had worked in the same accountancy firm for five years and had been promoted twice. As a manager, she now had an office on the first floor, which housed a large desk, two chairs and a meeting table. She felt proud that she had achieved this level of responsibility and that her hard work in studying for additional qualifications had paid off. Suzie also liked the fact that her office was slightly larger than the other offices on this floor, which she felt was a sign of her status.

At the monthly managers meeting she was told that change was afoot. The firm had decided to move to a flexible working environment because many people were now working in different locations including working from home. As a result, Suzie would no longer have an office. Instead, she could work from a workstation and when meetings were scheduled the quiet rooms could be booked for this purpose. It would mean a bit of chaos while the changes were implemented, but things would be better in the long term. The directors thought that everyone would be pleased, but not so. Suzie was upset: she had worked so hard to be recognized as a manager who had an office, and now it was to be taken away from her. She reacted negatively to this announcement at the meeting and became highly demotivated.

A simple change of environment at work had the potential to demotivate a member of staff. However, it was not the change itself – the real issue was the loss of status (esteem) for Suzie. It might have been quite different for another member of the team who felt more motivated because they could work from home more easily. It would have been far more motivating for Suzie if the director had talked to her separately and reinforced how much she was valued in the organization, and work out with her how her status needs could be met in light of the changes.

Motive for action = To save money and have a flexible workspace

Behaviour = Managers told they no longer have offices

Result = Loss of esteem and status for Suzie, leading to her becoming demotivated

Additional need = Suzie needs to be recognized in other ways

We need to remember that not everyone is motivated by the same things. At various points in their lives and careers, people will be motivated by completely different needs. It is imperative that you identify what the needs of each person are at any particular time. Here are some ways to apply Maslow's theory at work:

- **Physiological needs** Provide ample breaks for lunch and recuperation, and pay salaries that ensure that workers can buy life's essentials.
- **Safety needs** Provide a working environment that is safe, as well as job security and freedom from threats.
- **Social needs** Generate a feeling of acceptance, belonging and community by encouraging team working.
- **Esteem needs** Recognize achievements, assign important projects and provide status to make employees feel valued and appreciated.
- **Self-actualization** Offer challenging and meaningful work assignments that enable innovation, creativity and progress according to long-term goals.

McClelland's Human Motivation Theory

Finally today, now that you have learned about Herzberg's and Maslow's theories and worked out your Meta Programs by thinking about what type of language motivates you, you can complete your learning by understanding the theory developed by David McClelland about human motivation.

What his research identified was that there are three motivators that we all have – **achievement**, **affiliation** and **power** – and that each of us will display different characteristics depending on our dominant motivator, which has been shaped by our background, culture and life experiences. The table below summarizes the characteristics of each type of person.

McClelland's dominant motivators

Dominant motivator	Characteristics of the person
Achievement	• Has a need to set and achieve challenging goals • Likes to take risks to achieve their goals • Enjoys getting feedback on progress towards their goals • Often prefers to work alone
Affiliation	• Has a need to be liked and to be part of a group • May tend to go along with what others want in order to maintain harmony and good relations in a group • Does not enjoy risk taking and uncertainty
Power	• Enjoys having power and influence over others • Enjoys competing and winning • Likes recognition and status

You can observe people displaying these different needs in lots of team situations. For example, a group of friends went on a skiing holiday together. Those who had a strong **need for achievement** were focused on discovering the new ski routes they could tackle every day, and were keen to try some of the more difficult runs as soon as they could. They were not bothered if others in the group preferred to ski on easier runs and would arrange to catch up with them at lunchtime or at the end of the day.

Those with a **need for affiliation** would go along with what the majority agreed to do, whether or not they really were keen to do it. So they would often spend quite a bit of time during the day stopping for refreshments and enjoying the conversations with their friends. And those with a **need for power** were the ones that tended to organize the plan each morning and work out what they thought each person should do. They would also encourage competition on the slopes to see who could ski fastest down a particular run.

Think about groups or teams you have been in before and what behaviour you displayed. Which need drives you – power, affiliation or achievement?

Summary

Today you have discovered more about what drives you. This is important because, in order to be able to inspire and motivate others, you need to start by being motivated yourself. This can come from within you (intrinsic motivation) or it can be encouraged by some type of external reward (e.g. money, recognition). Remember that, if you want people to be motivated for a long period of time, the drive must come from within them.

We also looked at concepts related to motivation, including Meta Programs and theories developed by Herzberg, Maslow and McClelland. These help you to make sense of why individuals behave in particular ways at work and what some of the often unconscious intentions behind their actions are. Tomorrow you will learn how to use this knowledge to help you work out how to manage other people.

SUNDAY

MONDAY

TUESDAY

WEDNESDAY

THURSDAY

FRIDAY

SATURDAY

Fact-check (answers at the back)

1. Long-term motivation should come from:
   a) External sources (e.g. money) ❑
   b) Within yourself ❑
   c) Your manager ❑
   d) Being recognized ❑

2. According to a survey in *The Times*, the main reason people leave their jobs is:
   a) Lack of stimulus and no opportunity for advancement ❑
   b) Lack of a salary increase ❑
   c) They don't like their manager ❑
   d) They don't have a reason ❑

3. Herzberg's theory states that people needs are ultimately satisfied when:
   a) Their extrinsic needs are met ❑
   b) Their intrinsic needs are met ❑
   c) They like the team they are working in ❑
   d) Both their extrinsic and intrinsic needs are met ❑

4. An effective way to discover the Meta Programs that other people use to filter out information is to:
   a) Ask them ❑
   b) Go on a training course ❑
   c) Listen to the language that they use ❑
   d) Use the Meta Programs app ❑

5. The opposite end of the spectrum in the Meta Program 'Towards and _____' is:
   a) Avoiding ❑
   b) Away From ❑
   c) Specific ❑
   d) Difference ❑

6. In Maslow's Hierarchy of Needs, the second highest level of need is:
   a) Self-actualization ❑
   b) Social needs ❑
   c) Esteem needs ❑
   d) Physiological needs ❑

7. According to Maslow, if someone believes their job security is threatened, what is this level of needs?
   a) Self-actualization ❑
   b) Social ❑
   c) Esteem ❑
   d) Safety ❑

8. The three dominant motivators McClelland identified are affiliation, power and:
   a) Achievement ❑
   b) Loyalty ❑
   c) Belonging ❑
   d) Esteem ❑

9. According to McClelland's theory, someone who enjoys competition and winning is driven by a need for:
   a) Affiliation ❑
   b) Power ❑
   c) Belonging ❑
   d) Achievement ❑

10. If you provide ample breaks for lunch and recuperation, and pay decent salaries, you are addressing what level of need, according to Maslow?
   a) Security ❑
   b) Social ❑
   c) Self-actualization ❑
   d) Esteem ❑

MONDAY

TUESDAY

WEDNESDAY

THURSDAY

FRIDAY

SATURDAY

MONDAY

Stepping into their world

Yesterday you established in your mind what your motivations are. It is now time to take a step into the world of other people and work out what motivates them.

Why? Because it is only when you begin to understand someone by 'stepping into their shoes' that you discover what is likely to motivate and encourage them, and what may be less effective. That might seem like a lot of effort, but it is definitely worth while.

Often, people who are managers make the mistake of assuming that other people are 'just like them' and then try to use the same approach that works for them personally. Or they think that, because it worked with their previous team, it will work again with their new team. This generally does not take into consideration that another person might have different perspectives based on age, gender, culture, background, experience, interests and so on. A 'one size motivates all' approach is unlikely to work.

Today you will be able to develop a framework that will help you to analyse those you need to motivate, by using the theories learned on Sunday and a few other important techniques. This will help you to develop personalized strategies for those people you have to motivate to achieve specific goals or tasks, and begin to recognize what is working or what changes in your approach you may need to make.

Taking time to understand other people will help you to build better rapport and trust, and therefore to have a greater likelihood of positively influencing them to achieve the results you want.

> Remember the question that is likely to be in a person's mind is:
> 'What's in it for me?'

Generational differences at work

The labour force is now made up of a number of different generations and it is useful to consider this when working out what is likely to motivate particular individuals. Each of these generations has gone through different experiences in their lifetimes which influence their behaviour and expectations.

- Traditionalists (born 1922–43)
- Baby Boomers (born 1943–60)
- Generation X (born 1960–80)
- Millennials or Generation Y (born 1980–2000)

Today's youngest employees are likely to have quite a different set of perspectives, expectations and outlook compared to those who are older, such as Generation X and Baby Boomers. Some of the characteristics that define each generation are in the table below.

These characteristics can affect behaviour at work and an example of this would be in providing feedback, which is a very useful tool in encouraging motivation. If you were to categorize how the different generations perceive feedback, it might be described as:

- **Traditionalists:** 'No news is good news.'
- **Baby Boomers:** 'Get feedback once a year and lots of documentation.'
- **Generation X:** 'Sorry to interrupt, but how am I doing?'
- **Millennials:** 'Feedback whenever I want it at the push of a button.'

Generational characteristics

Generation	Characteristics
Traditionalists (born 1922–43) *Experienced World War II*	Hard work Dedication and sacrifice Respect for rules Duty before pleasure Honour
Baby Boomers (born 1943–1960) *Era of civil rights, Women's Movement,* *Man on the moon, Cold War,* *Woodstock*	Optimism Team orientation Personal gratification Involvement Personal growth Values
Generation X (born 1960–80) *MTV generation, Thatcher era in UK,* *Reagan era in US*	Diversity Techno-literacy Fun and informality Self-reliance Pragmatism
Millennials (Generation Y) (born 1980–2000) *September 11th Attacks, digital* *technology, pressure to excel*	Optimism Feel civic duty Confidence Achievement orientation Respect for diversity

So the style that might be appealing and helpful to one generation may seem too formal and advisory to another. For example, traditionalists are unlikely to seek out recognition but will appreciate acknowledgement that they have made a difference. The next generation, Baby Boomers, are more used to giving feedback, but less used to receiving it, especially positive feedback, and may appear uncomfortable. The Generation X workers need plenty of positive feedback to encourage them, and the Millennials need much more instant feedback to ensure that they know what they are doing right and what they are doing wrong.

If you are motivating people who are of a different generation to you, it is useful to pay attention to what their expectations may be in terms of feedback and recognition. There is more detail on the subject of recognition and appreciation on Friday.

The impact of values on behaviour

Values are another factor that affect how individuals behave. Values drive our behaviour, and in the workplace it's far easier to motivate staff if you are able to align their personal values with those of the organization.

Values are the rules that we live our lives by and define who we are. For example, if one of your core values is 'family', and you have to work 70 hours per week, it's likely that you will feel internal stress and conflict because you are not being able to spend time with your family.

To think about what your values are, you can ask yourself 'What is important in my work...?' or read the list of values below and identify which ones are important to you. Add in others if your priorities are not listed. If you are not sure, then think about situations where you have felt strongly about something – it's likely that your values were challenged at that time. For example, if you value honesty and are then asked to carry out a task at work that requires you to be dishonest, it is likely that this was challenging one of your values.

- Accomplishment
- Accuracy
- Adventure
- Authenticity
- Being known
- Collaboration
- Community
- Empowerment
- Excellence
- Fairness
- Family
- Freedom
- Friendship
- Fun
- Giving
- Harmony
- Helping others
- Honesty
- Humour
- Independence
- Integrity
- Joy
- Love
- Nurturing
- Order
- Participation
- Peace
- Performance
- Recognition
- Respect
- Reward
- Service
- Sharing
- Status
- Success

Then ask yourself: 'If I had all of these values at work, what would make me leave?' This might generate some other values. To put them in order of priority, look at the first two values on your list and ask yourself, 'If I could satisfy only one of these, which would I choose?' Continue on through the list until you have put them in order. Once you know what your core values are, it's far easier to make decisions about how you live your life and what career you follow.

As a manager, it helps to understand what the values are of those you need to motivate. You can do this by asking them, or by noticing how they behave in particular situations. Then, if you are able to create a connection between the values that an individual has and the organization's values, it is much more powerful in building motivation.

Case study: conflicting values

Bogusia is the manager of a team in a fast-growing technology company. Her experience in this case study is a good example of how individual values can become conflicted in a team. She values hard work and as a result is normally first to arrive and last to leave the office. Bogusia judges other people in a similar way and therefore thinks that Ethan is not committed because he tends to leave work most days around 17.30.

Ethan has 'family' as one of his core values and believes that he can do a good day's work and ensure that he gets home in time to spend time with his family, too. Often, he will deal with emails and last-minute issues after his children have gone to bed, so he works flexibly, which Bogusia is not aware of. It is only when she has a conversation with Ethan that she realizes that this is the case.

What Bogusia needs to learn is to accept that other people may have different values and priorities to her, but that they can still deliver the results that the company requires.

Ethan's motive for action = Fulfil values – to spend time with family

> **Behaviour** = Works in evenings but leaves office at 17.30 every day
>
> **Result** = Manager challenges Ethan's commitment – but he is happier because he is living in accordance with his values
>
> **Additional benefit** = Prompts conversation between manager and Ethan regarding hours worked versus results achieved

By now, you are probably beginning to build up a picture of how complicated it can be to work out what drives the behaviour of any individual. It can be influenced by a myriad of different things, but the more you pay attention to the subtleties of language and actions, the easier it is to work out how to effectively influence and motivate others. Of course, an individual's personality will be another facet of how they behave, and it's worth having a basic understanding of different personality types so that you can readily identify characteristics that affect their behaviour.

Personality types

Historically, there are four temperaments that people display:

- **Sanguine** pleasure-seeking and sociable
- **Choleric** ambitious and leader-like
- **Melancholic** introverted and thoughtful
- **Phlegmatic** relaxed and quiet

Carl Jung's work built on these temperaments to identify the difference between extravert and introvert personality types, which was then the basis for the creation of the well-known personality inventory, the Myers-Briggs Type Indicator® (MBTI), developed by Katherine Cook Briggs and her daughter Isabel Briggs Myers. This type of personality assessment is a practical way to help people in a team to understand more about themselves and their colleagues, and can be used to generate motivation in a team. This psychometric tool is administered by those who are qualified MBTI assessors.

The MBTI shows that there are four different spectrums highlighting the preferences that someone has in:

- being energized
- receiving information
- making decisions
- living their life.

Just like the Meta Programs described on Sunday, people have a preference for either one or the other of a pair (e.g. Sensing or Intuition).

MBTI personality types

Being energized	
E *Extraversion*	**I** *Introversion*
Likes to talk things through	Likes to think things through
Receiving information	
S *Sensing*	**N** *Intuition*
Pays attention to the facts and details	Can see the big picture and possibilities
Making decisions	
T *Thinking*	**F** *Feeling*
Considers situations using logic	Considers others before making decisions
Living your life	
J *Judging*	**P** *Perceiving*
Enjoys routine and to-do lists	Loves the joy of keeping options open

While everyone has the capability to adapt to all the different styles, we all tend to have four particular preferences – e.g. Extraversion (E), Intuition (N), Feeling (F), Judging (J) – which gives a four-letter descriptor for their type (in this case it is ENFJ). These different types, when described in more detail, can help people in a team, as well as the manager or leader, to understand how their preferences can influence behaviour in a team.

Some ways that these MBTI preferences show up at work are described below.

Working on an individual project

If you ask a person who has an Extraversion preference
to work alone for a few days on a project, they are likely to
become demotivated fairly quickly because they thrive on being
energized by other people. This would not bother those with an
Introversion preference quite so much.

Ideas for the future

If you want to quickly engage someone with a Sensing
preference, then ensure that you have all the facts and data
at your disposal so that they can consider the concrete
details on the project. However, if you want ideas for future
improvements, then you can motivate someone who has an
Intuition preference as they are more likely to be energized by
thinking about future possibilities.

Considering the facts in making a decision

An organization that is cutting back its workforce has a
meeting to discuss the action plan. The people with the
Thinking preference are more likely to have considered all the
logical reasons (e.g. cost saving, increased efficiencies, how
to create a plan, etc.). Those with a Feeling preference tend to
find it easier to think about how the others might feel about
the situation, and what should be done to maintain harmony
during times of change. Both approaches are required and
equally beneficial for the success of the project.

Last-minute preparation

Two team members, Scott and Mary Lou, were preparing to
run a course together. Scott, with the Judging preference,
had the programme planned a month ahead so that he felt
organized and in control. However, he could not get Mary Lou
(with a Perceiving preference) to do anything this far ahead.
She became focused with three days to go, and then rushed
around ensuring that all the final details were correct. When
they found that the client had also made some last-minute

changes to the programme, this did not bother Mary Lou, whereas Scott was frustrated that it was all being left to the last minute and then being changed. However, over time he learned to relax and trust that Mary Lou would cope with the changes and keep him posted.

You can also see below the effect when you add some of the preferences together and how this can impact on behaviour.

- **IS Type** People who are energized by their inner world and have a Sensing preference are motivated by maintaining continuity – *'Let's keep things the same.'*
- **IN Type** People who are energized by their inner world and have an Intuition preference are motivated by thinking through ideas for the future – *'Let's think about possibilities.'*
- **ES Type** People who are energized by the outer world and have a Sensing preference are motivated by action and results which help tasks to be more efficient – *'Let's take action.'*
- **ES Type** People who are energized by the outer world and have an Intuition preference are motivated by change and trying something different or new – *'Let's change it.'*

Recognition and appreciation

The way that someone likes to be recognized or appreciated is quite different for a person with a Thinking preference (T) compared to someone with a Feeling preference (F). Try it out for yourself. Answer the questions below:

- Which word do you prefer – recognition or appreciation?
- What do you like to be recognized or appreciated for?
- How do you like to be recognized or appreciated?
- What happens if you are not recognized or appreciated in this way?

Based on research from Myers-Briggs Type Indicator (in the OPP Myers – Briggs Type Indicator Assessor Training Programme), the way that someone is recognized or appreciated can have a profound effect on their motivation. See the table below.

Recognition or appreciation?

Question	Thinking types (T)	Feeling types (F)
Which word do you prefer?	• Recognized	• Appreciated
How do you like to be recognized/appreciated?	• By someone I respect • Not too effusively • With money • By being given a larger project	• With personal and genuine thanks • With plenty of appreciation • Must be sincere • Tokens and gestures
What do you like to be recognized/appreciated for?	• For a job well done – achieving an outcome • Not just for an average job • Task-oriented achievement	• A personal contribution • Making a difference because of who I am • Helping others practically
What if you are not recognized/appreciated in this way?	• Get angry or annoyed ('I'll show them') • Reduced input • 'It's their problem not mine' • Feeling down for a short time, but will get over it	• Feel hurt • Become demotivated • Lose confidence • 'What did I do wrong?' • Can have a profound effect and could lead to leaving job

As a team leader or manager, it is vital that you don't just 'do unto others as you would like done to you' because it could demotivate those who are different from you. If you heap praise for a routine piece of work on a person with a Thinking preference, they are likely to think it is patronizing, particularly if it is not given by someone they respect. And then if you make them stand out in front of all their colleagues to be recognized, that is even worse! You could get the best out of them by focusing on what they have achieved that required real effort, and then give them even more work as a reward.

Beliefs drive behaviour

However, there may be some people that you find it difficult to work with, and it can be even more challenging when you have to work with them to achieve an outcome. For example, your perception of an individual is that they are always rude to people who are more junior than them. The important thing to remember is that your beliefs about them will drive your behaviour and you might end up not getting your need met.

Your belief – 'I don't respect this person.'

Your feelings – You feel annoyed and irritated.

Behaviour – You treat them in an offhand manner.

Outcome – They ignore your request and you don't get the task completed on time.

So, if you want to achieve a different outcome, it might mean changing your beliefs about them. Remember, a belief is *not* a fact. It is something that you accept as true or real, and which drives your behaviour.

You might have to accept that in order to get the task completed you need to change your belief about that person. Remember that we are all motivated by two things:

1 the strength of our needs
2 the perception that taking an action will satisfy those needs.

So, if your need is to motivate a person to achieve a task, and your belief or perception is that no matter much you stress the importance of the deadline, they won't achieve it, that is likely to be the outcome you will get. If the need is strong enough, you will probably be motivated to change your belief and adopt a different approach in order to get the outcome you want.

Accepting, not agreeing...
If you accept that another person has a different set of beliefs from you, that does not mean that you are agreeing with them, only accepting that they are different. This is a key point to pay attention to.

Summary

Today you have gained insights into what drives others and the significance that values and personality preferences can have. When you add these elements to the theories and models on motivation described yesterday, you should have a better appreciation of what to pay attention to when observing behaviour.

The key to being able to motivate other people is to be able to step into their world and understand what it's like for that individual and what is driving them. Once you take the time to do this, and examine what is really going on for that person, and why they behave as they do, then it is like putting the pieces of a jigsaw together to create a clearer picture of the situation.

The exciting part is then using the information to decide on what strategy you will employ to motivate them.

SUNDAY

MONDAY

TUESDAY

WEDNESDAY

THURSDAY

FRIDAY

SATURDAY

Fact-check (answers at the back)

1. What is likely to be the key question in the mind of the individual you are seeking to motivate?
   a) 'What's in it for me?' ☐
   b) 'When do we begin?' ☐
   c) 'How much do I get paid?' ☐
   d) 'Who is in the team?' ☐

2. Millennials expect to receive feedback:
   a) Rarely and with lots of documentation ☐
   b) When they have done something wrong ☐
   c) Whenever they want it, at the push of a button ☐
   d) Only if it is positive ☐

3. Generation X...
   a) Are generally optimistic ☐
   b) Feel a sense of duty before pleasure ☐
   c) Are achievement-oriented ☐
   d) Are highly literate with technology ☐

4. One way to identify what your values are is to:
   a) Think about what you feel strongly about ☐
   b) Go on a training course ☐
   c) Speak to your manager and ask them ☐
   d) Keep asking the question 'Why?' ☐

5. Respect, honesty, family and excellence are all examples of:
   a) Values ☐
   b) Motivational theories ☐
   c) 1980s bands ☐
   d) Teams in your organization ☐

6. Which of the following is *not* one of the four temperaments?
   a) Phlegmatic – relaxed and quiet ☐
   b) Careful – thoughtful and detailed ☐
   c) Sanguine – pleasure-seeking and sociable ☐
   d) Choleric – ambitious and leader-like ☐

7. According to the Myers-Briggs Type Indicator, people who are energized by the outer world and have a Sensing preference are more likely to say:
   a) 'Let's keep things the same.' ☐
   b) 'Let's take action.' ☐
   c) 'Let's think differently.' ☐
   d) 'Let's improve things.' ☐

8. People who are Thinking types like to be recognized:
   a) Because of who they are ☐
   b) By being given less work ☐
   c) With genuine appreciation ☐
   d) By money and for a job well done ☐

9. If a Feeling type person is not appreciated over a long period of time, they are likely to:
   a) Have a loss of confidence ☐
   b) Feel down, but get over it ☐
   c) Get angry ☐
   d) Not be bothered ☐

10. A belief is:
    a) A fact ☐
    b) Something that you accept as true or real ☐
    c) A motivational theory ☐
    d) A value ☐

TUESDAY

Motivation vs. inspiration

It's Tuesday and by now you'll have a better idea of what motivates you and some fundamental principles of motivation. Now it's time to clarify your thinking on how you can motivate those you work with.

No matter whether you are a manager, leader or team member or you work on your own, you will have to interact with other people. Therefore it is important to influence others positively. Today we will explore a number of ways in which you can do that:

1 Communication – understanding how, why, when, where, what, and which style to inspire or motivate
2 Decision-making – logic vs. emotion
3 Role models – becoming a catalyst or exemplar for change
4 Self-Determination Theory – helping to encourage autonomy

Being inspirational

So what is the difference between motivation and inspiration? The simple answer is a lot!

The *Merriam-Webster Collegiate Dictionary* provides the following definitions:

Motivation The reason or reasons one has for acting or behaving in a particular way.

Inspiration The process of being mentally stimulated to do or feel something.

If you have to motivate others, it's likely that you will have to be inspired and motivated yourself, as well as possibly being a role model for them. Consider the following questions:

- Do you expect that a leader or manager should be a role model?
- What does a role model mean to you?
- Given that anyone can be a role model, how do you motivate or inspire others?
- For whom might you already be a role model or inspiration? (You do not necessarily have to work with them.)

These questions, as well as the key learning points below, will be addressed today as we explore how you can motivate and inspire people to achieve organizational and business goals.

> *'Motivation is the art of getting people to do what you want them to do because they want to do it.'*
>
> Dwight D. Eisenhower

Think about a leader who has inspired you in the past. It might be someone you have worked for, read about or seen on television. What is it about them that inspired you? This might give you some ideas on what you can do, or are already doing, that might be inspiring to others.

It's part of the job

Providing inspiration as a manager or leader is not just an extra part of your job. It is an essential element.

Research carried out by John Zenger, Joseph Folkman and Scott Edinger over a four-year period to determine what makes an outstanding leader showed that the ability to 'inspire and motivate high performance' was the single most powerful predictor of being perceived as an extraordinary leader.

Here are some examples of things you can do become a more inspiring leader or manager:

- **Practise effective communication** – you will learn more about how to do this over the next few pages.
- **Be the example** – show by your actions that you put into practice the behaviours that are valued by the organization. Be prepared to set challenging goals yourself and 'walk your talk'.
- **Spend time with those you manage.** View your job as enabling your people to succeed, which means you have to support and encourage them.
- **Delegate tasks with the development of the other person in mind.** Ask yourself: 'Is this task an opportunity for someone to develop their skills in — ?'
- **Get around.** Take the time to walk around and speak to people; don't just send them an email.
- **Recognize others.** Show genuine appreciation and enthusiasm, and remember to pay attention to the different preferences that were outlined on Monday.

- **Show humility.** The ability to be humble and not arrogant is something that leaders and managers should develop, as it helps to build trust and acceptance.
- **Be a positive influence.** Practise being positive; do not fall into the trap of only being positive when something good or really important has happened. Instead, make being positive your new behaviour because, if you do it regularly, it will become a habit.
- **Provide social support.** Help your colleagues and do more than just show interest in them and their work.
- **Change your attitude to stress.** Stress is inevitable, so think of it as being more positive than negative.

Inspire, then motivate

If you put into practice some of the behaviours above, it's likely that, over time, you will be inspiring other people because they will see that you really want to help them succeed. That inspiration can turn to motivation within them, and as a result they will want to perform the action or task you want them to achieve – and to do so to the best of their ability.

Of course, it's not always easy. You may have to help them to be tenacious and maintain performance and motivation when they find it difficult. This is where being an inspiration can really bring benefits. All too often, the misapprehension is that 'being an inspiration' is the role of iconic leaders who are great orators and have 'presence' or charisma. While it is true that these aspects are important, the ability to be inspirational is not the sole preserve of a few.

Communication

As was mentioned already, how you communicate with people has a direct influence on how you are perceived by others, and the degree to which they are motivated. On Sunday you learned about Meta Programs, which can help you work out the language you should use.

The next step is to consider other people's communication preferences. An effective way to work this out is to draw on knowledge gained through NLP (neuro linguistic programming) – an approach developed by Richard Bandler and John Grinder.

Human beings experience the world through the physical senses. These are described as the **representational system** and they can be split into three groups:

1 **Visual** – the things we see
2 **Auditory** – the things we hear
3 **Kinaesthetic** – the things we feel (touch/emotion), taste and smell.

Your brain uses your senses to build your **internal representation**, or model, of the world around you.

Read the explanation of the preferences below (which are adapted from Tony Nutley, UK College of Personal Development, NLP Programme) and identify which one appeals to you most. This will help you work out your preferred representational system.

Visual

'If I could show you a really brilliant way of communicating that could make you appear more attractive to visionary people, you would at least want to look at it, wouldn't you?'

The benefits of building rapport with people who have a preference for the visual representational system is that it becomes so much clearer to see the way they view the world. It is when you see how things look from other points of view that you catch sight of the bigger picture. From this perspective, it is easier to see the way forward to a really bright future.

Auditory

'If I were to tell you about a way of communicating with people that would really want to make them prick up their ears and listen, you would at least want to hear about it, wouldn't you?'

Striking a harmonious chord with someone with an auditory preference might sound easy, and being in tune with them means that you are talking their language.

Kinaesthetic

'If I were to give you a really concrete way to get in touch with people, so that you can build rapport at a really deep level and get to grips with the way they hold reality, you would at least want to get a feel for it, wouldn't you?'

When you find common ground with people, you may feel that things move along more smoothly, that new connections are being made and that the path ahead becomes a stroll in the park.

Building rapport

By understanding your own preferred representational system, it can help you to work out why it might seem easier to communicate with some people than others. And for those that you find it more difficult to talk to, if you begin to notice which system they tend to use, you can notice how they react to you. If you then adapt how you communicate, it is likely that you'll have a better chance of building rapport with them.

Another element of communication that is helpful to be aware of is to pick up some of the non-verbal changes that happen in the person you are speaking to.

Case study: using sensory acuity

Sergey was asking a member of his team for an update on a task he had been given to complete. While the individual explained that progress was being made, and that it should be finished by the agreed deadline, the person's non-verbal communication told a different story.

Sergey couldn't help noticing that he was fidgeting and would not look directly at him. He spoke more quickly than usual and his face was reddening. So Sergey calmly enquired: 'Although you tell me everything is OK, my sense is that something's not right, because you are a bit agitated. Is there a problem?' At that point the person confessed that he was a bit unsure about one element of

The table below shows the key physical signs to be alert to:

Sensory acuity

Senses	Signs	Senses	Signs
Voice	Tone/pitch/pace	**Facial movements**	Eyebrows, muscle twitching
Skin tone	Colour and/or shininess	**Lip size**	Thinning
Eye movements	Up/down, left/right combinations	**Head**	Angle
Pupil of eye	Dilation or widening	**Physical gestures**	Hand/arm/foot/leg movements, fidgeting

Remember that few, if any, of the above signals 'mean' anything on their own. Reading body language is not about learning to attach some arbitrary meaning to each of the above, but to consider them along with all the other information you are getting from another person.

Communication methods in business

As a manager who wants to inspire or motivate others, you are likely to be under time pressure to get tasks completed. There can be a temptation to use the quickest method, which might not always be the most effective.

So make sure you have thought through which method(s) are best for the particular person you are motivating. Some people prefer to communicate by email, which can allow time for thinking and reflection, whereas others thrive on the stimulus of regular face-to-face contact.

In today's world a simple representation of communication methods is:

- **One-dimensional (1D) communication = written (e.g. SMS text, email, Internet)**
  The vocabulary used and construction of the words within the communication are what will convey meaning. However, this can be misinterpreted as the initiator is not present so cannot use the other senses to gauge the person's situation or mood, and cannot make adjustments to the communication 'in the moment'.
- **Two-dimensional (2D) communication = verbal (e.g. telephone, Skype call)**
  Through the tone, pace and volume of voice, those present in the call can better evaluate the communication, ask questions to clarify understanding and make adjustments. Both parties will gain more meaning than in a written (1D) communication
- **Three-dimensional (3D) communication = in person (i.e. meeting someone face to face)**
  Visual conference calls could be regarded as 2D rather than as 3D, although advances in technology and greater familiarity with it may change this view. In this mode, there is the full range of conscious communications taking place, plus other subtler subconscious non-verbal signals (e.g. body language).

The most effective form of communication is 3D and the most convenient is 1D. Emails, SMS texts and social media are the most popular forms of communication now, and with them often comes the expectation of a rapid response, which can cause people problems as they send messages without fully thinking them through.

Gauging what and when to communicate is a critical success factor in influencing others. So, when you want to motivate or inspire someone else, think about which communication mode you should use and remember to pay close attention to the state the recipient is in and the representational system that works best for them.

Logic vs. emotion

Think of a situation where you had a bulletproof case or justification for an action and where the facts, the reasons and logic behind it were clear. Yet the other person dug their heels in and refused to budge. Your logic did not succeed.

Decision-making is invariably emotional rather than just purely logical – through neuroscience the reasons for this are becoming better understood. Decisions are made by not just working out the pros and cons, but also relying on feelings, which some may describe as using their instincts.

If you want to successfully influence others, then using the organization's goals and values as the sole reason for action may not be enough. It is better to help others discover for themselves what feels right, too. This may involve spending some time with them building up their trust in you. By understanding their situation (e.g. their problems, concerns and objectives), you can indicate that what *you* want to achieve, can also help *them* with the issues they have. In other words, you achieve a win-win outcome.

One way to try to access people's emotions is to ask open-ended questions, as these will help to get someone talking and expressing themselves. It encourages the person to begin a dialogue and so set the course of the conversation, which can help them to start feeling safer and achieving greater self-expression.

Examples of open-ended questions

'What is bothering you?' ('Is something bothering you?' is an example of a closed question and one that is likely to result in a one-word answer!)

'What would you like to talk about?'

'What's been happening since we last met?'

'How do you think this could be improved?'

'What makes you think it may be time for this to be changed?'

Practising asking open questions could prove helpful. However, be aware that, if you use this approach too often or in the wrong circumstances, you could be viewed as indecisive or as a procrastinator. In this situation, you should switch to using closed questions that encourage a 'yes' or 'no' answer, and help someone to commit to an action.

Examples of closed questions

'Are you going to complete the report by tomorrow?'

'Have you managed to work out a solution to this?'

'Is Mary attending the meeting, too?'

So now you are likely to have a greater awareness of the nuances of communication that can make a difference in how you motivate people. Take time to observe, and to practise behaviours that are different from your normal preferences.

Role models

If you have a leadership or management role in an organization, then you will be aware that your staff tends to take their cues as to how to behave based on what they observe you doing. So are you behaving as a role model?

What does a role model mean to you?
Who are your role models?
Why are they role models?

As well as being a role model, you may find it very helpful to have role models whom you can learn from and aspire to be. A lot can be gained by studying others and, if possible, by discussing their careers and decisions with them. People are often flattered when others ask them for help, so don't be afraid to do so.

> ## Positive energy
>
> Both motivation and inspiration require positive energy, and by developing positive habits of nurturing, supporting and recognizing the efforts of others you will discover new levels of pleasure in how you work, which are likely to be mirrored by those who work with you.

 Keep your integrity
Be mindful of not becoming so agile and adaptable that what you say or do becomes an 'act'. If you adapt yourself too much, you are likely to dilute your values to a point you do not really believe in what you are saying or doing. This runs the risk of being considered disingenuous.

Self-Determination Theory

Traditional thinking has been that motivation in the workplace is driven by external reward; more recently, recognition has also been added to the mix. This has led to quantity becoming the focus – that is, 'more is better'. Over the last 40 years important work done by psychologists and neuroscientists has given us a better understanding of motivation that challenges this thinking.

Two research psychologists, Edward Deci and Richard Ryan, have developed their Self Determination Theory, in which they propose the importance of the *quality* of motivation over the *quantity* of motivation. A central theme to their view is that there are two types of motivation – **controlled** and **autonomous**.

Controlled and autonomous motivation

	Approach	Method	Effect
Controlled motivation ('carrot and stick')			
	Seduce	Reward	Pressure
	Coerce	Threat	Pressure
Autonomous motivation ('self-determination')			
	Choice	Inclusion	Willingness
	Endorsement	Support	Enjoyment
	Interest	Belief	Feeling valued

The benefits of autonomous motivation are that it leads to better creativity, problem solving, task performance and a positive emotional state. These benefits are achieved because the person has:

- had their own perspective / internal frame of reference considered
- been engaged in the decision-making process
- been shown a willingness to explore new ways
- discovered a higher level of 'self-starter' energy within themselves
- found the rationale behind what is meaningful (i.e., related to their values and beliefs)
- gained a sense of enjoyment through the approach.

Deci and Ryan's Self-Determination Theory is a theory of motivation that aims to explain individuals' goal-directed behaviour. They believe that motivation resides along a continuum, with intrinsic motivation on the far right, extrinsic motivation in the middle and amotivation on the far left – which is a state of lacking any motivation to engage in an activity (being apathetic):

**Deci and Ryan's
motion continuum**

AMOTIVATION	EXTRINSIC MOTIVATION	INTRINSIC MOTIVATION
Lacking motivation to engage in activity	Motivation from external factors	Motivation from 'within'

The critical component of the theory concerns the degree to which individuals fulfil their basic psychological needs. So the more someone attains these needs, the more their behaviour is self-determined. The three main psychological needs they identified are:

1 **autonomy**
2 **competence**
3 **relatedness**.

'Motivation is the energy for action.'
Edward Deci

How to encourage autonomy

So how do you encourage autonomy while ensuring that the goals of the organization are met? Here are some guidelines adapted from Ryan and Deci:

- **Share decision-making.** This is not practical in all circumstances, but it is in more cases than we often assume. If goals are non-negotiable, allow people to determine how they will get there. The more people participate in the decisions that affect them, the more engaged they will be.
- **Explain the reasons for goals and rules.** Take time to explain why a rule exists, or how a task is important to a larger objective, as it helps to encourage engagement.
- **Adopt the other's perspective.** Once you understand another person's perspective, it's easier to work out – together – how you might help achieve the organizational goals.

● **Foster an alliance.** Hierarchical relationships have their place, but work-related or behaviour-related goals are often shared. The manager is not responsible for an employee's mistakes, but they are responsible for the final product. Make your mutual interest clear – as well as your offer of support.

Summary

Motivation, as Edward Deci writes, is 'energy for action' and it comes from within, and if you want to influence another person's motivation you have to appeal to them at a logical and an emotional level.

Inspiration is built upon positive energy, an appealing vision and compelling behaviour. Through your behaviour you can inspire other people. You may not think that it is your job to inspire others, but do not underestimate the positive effect it can have on other people. They may never tell you, but you will know it by the way they behave towards you.

In order to motivate or inspire, you will need to positively influence others and be able to assess and react to a situation well. You also need to be agile in how you adapt your thinking, behaviour and communications to different people and situations.

To influence effectively is a skill that can be learned. The level to which one can influence is also a factor of your character. While you might argue that your character cannot be changed, it can be – if you want it to be. So you have to find the motivation – the reason from within that makes it worth while to change.

SUNDAY

MONDAY

TUESDAY

WEDNESDAY

THURSDAY

FRIDAY

SATURDAY

Fact-check (answers at the back)

1. Inspiration is:
   a) the process of being mentally stimulated to do or feel something ❏
   b) the reason or reasons one has for acting or behaving in a particular way ❏
   c) difficult to do if you are demotivated ❏
   d) something that only those with charisma can give ❏

2. What is an essential element of your job as a manager or leader?
   a) Using your mobile phone at the weekend ❏
   b) Keeping your salary confidential ❏
   c) Getting everyone a cup of coffee ❏
   d) Inspiring others ❏

3. Which answer below is *not* something you should do to become more inspiring?
   a) Spend time with those you manage ❏
   b) Show humility ❏
   c) Take all the credit for tasks your team achieve ❏
   d) Delegate tasks with the development of the other person in mind ❏

4. According to NLP, which of the following is *not* a representational system?
   a) Auditory ❏
   b) Kinaesthetic ❏
   c) Telepathic ❏
   d) Visual ❏

5. Meeting someone face to face would be an example of:
   a) 1D communication ❏
   b) 2D communication ❏
   c) 3D communication ❏
   d) 4D communication ❏

6. An example of an open-ended question is:
   a) 'What's been happening since we last met?' ❏
   b) 'Have you completed the report yet?' ❏
   c) 'Is George attending the meeting?' ❏
   d) 'Could you collect the manager from the station?' ❏

7. An example of a closed question is:
   a) 'How is the report progressing?' ❏
   b) 'Which option do you think is best for our office reorganization?' ❏
   c) 'What training requirements do you have for the next 12 months?' ❏
   d) 'Are you going to complete the report by tomorrow?' ❏

8. Becoming too agile and adaptable in your communication style could result in:
   a) You being clear about who 'you' really are ❏
   b) Being seen as weak ❏
   c) Spending a lot of time of this activity ❏
   d) Others seeing you as disingenuous and putting on an act ❏

9. Deci and Ryan's Self-Determination Theory states:
a) That the carrot-and-stick approach is a key facet ☐
b) That the more someone attains their basic psychological needs, the more their behaviour is self-determined ☐
c) That the three main psychological needs are power, affiliation and achievement ☐
d) That seducing and coercing are two approaches to use ☐

10. One effective way to encourage autonomy is:
a) Set ambitious goals ☐
b) Share decision-making ☐
c) Take responsibility for the employee's mistakes ☐
d) Use the carrot-and-stick approach ☐

WEDNESDAY

Taking the wider perspective

In order to develop your ability to influence and inspire others it is hugely important to look outside your 'local environment'. When looking further afield you can discover fresh ideas, new examples of best practice and gain a broader appreciation of the context in which you work. Invariably, the nuances that can improve things can be sensed only when you branch out further than the world in which you work. By doing this, you can put work pressures into a more meaningful perspective, which in turn can fuel your motivation and that of others with whom you work.

Today you will learn how to benefit from working in a matrix environment where you can find yourself working with people from other departments who have different skills and experiences from you. There may also be people who are more senior or junior to you in the organization, plus people from other organizations (e.g. suppliers, technical partners or clients) or from other countries, which introduces you to a range of different cultures.

Following on from this, we will also discuss the challenges of influencing, and being influenced by, other functions and disciplines in an organization. This will then take you into a brief exploration of the importance of organizational awareness and finding people who can support and work with you to achieve the results you need to deliver.

Maintaining motivation in a matrix world

When you are faced with the ever–increasing demands of organizational life, where matrix management, multiple projects, stretch goals and various other organizational initiatives and programmes can make working life quite challenging, it can be hard to maintain your own motivation, let alone think about being an inspiration to others.

Juggling priorities is hard enough, so when it is compounded by having to contend with changes that can come from outside your local world (e.g. from a person in a sister company or partnership business where you have no visibility in their world), it can be quite a surprise and a potential demotivator.

> *'People expect their leaders to help them to achieve the common task: To build the synergy of teamwork and to respond to individuals and meet their needs.'*
>
> John Adair

The work of John Adair offers two useful leadership concepts that can help you to understand and use techniques that will enhance your motivational skills in this type of environment.

1 Action-Centred Leadership

John Adair created an 'organizational needs' model that considers the effectiveness of a leader through three areas of need:

Type of function	Type of need
Task functions	Sense of direction
Team functions	Sense of belonging
Individual functions	Sense of identity

The model is known as Action-Centred Leadership. Below is a simple diagram of the model showing how the three needs and functions are related.

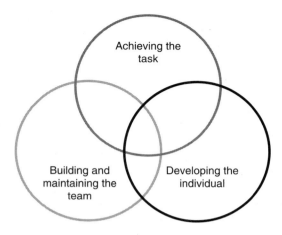

In order to help you relate the Action-Centred Leadership model to how you help motivate and inspire others, look at the sets of questions below, based on further work from John Adair. These will help you to analyse the way you can help to motivate the team you are part of, and then identify areas for improvement.

As you answer the questions, you might like to draw your own version of the model and consider:

- to what degree the circles overlap
- what are the causes of the overlaps
- actions you might wish to take to balance the model.

Action-Centred Leadership: checklists

Achieving the task		
Purpose:	Am I clear about what the task is?	
Responsibilities:	Am I clear what my responsibilities are?	
Objectives:	Have I agreed the objectives with my manager, or the person accountable for the group?	
Targets:	Has each team member clearly defined and agreed to the targets?	
Priorities:	Have I planned how to prioritize the time?	
Progress:	Do I check progress regularly, evaluate and encourage?	
Role model:	Do I set standards by my behaviour?	

Building and maintaining the team		
Objectives:	Does the team clearly understand and accept the objectives?	
Standards:	Do they know what standards of performance are expected?	
Team members:	Are the right people working together? Is there a need to create subgroups?	
Team spirit:	Do I look for opportunities for building teamwork into jobs? Do methods of pay and bonus help to develop team spirit?	
Consultation:	Is this genuine? Do I encourage and welcome ideas and suggestions? ·	
Briefing:	Is this regular? Does it cover current plans, progress and future developments?	
Support:	Do I see people at their work when the team is apart? Do I fairly represent the whole team in my manner and encouragement?	

Developing the individual		
Targets:	Have the targets been agreed and quantified with each individual?	
Achievement:	Does each person know how their work contributes to the overall result?	
Responsibilities:	Has each person got a clear and accurate job description? Can I delegate more to him/her?	
Authority:	Does she or he have sufficient authority for his/her task?	
Training:	Has adequate provision been made for training people in skills they require and about being a team member?	
Recognition:	Do I spend enough time with individuals listening and developing them? Do I recognize people's successes?	
Appraisal:	Is the overall performance of each individual regularly reviewed in a face-to-face discussion?	

Now that you have answered the questions, you might like to review whether:

- the Task/Team/Individual circles overlap sufficiently to provide and maintain morale in the face of difficult challenges
- there are adequate systems or procedures in place to resolve tensions and conflicts effectively.

2 Influencing across borders – the '50/50 Rule'

The second concept of John Adair's that is useful to remember is the 50/50 Rule – 50 per cent of motivation comes from within a person and 50 per cent from his or her environment, especially from the leadership encountered there. The rule, like the popular management tool known as the Pareto Principle (commonly known as the '80/20 Rule'), provides a very useful guideline.

When trying to motivate others, it is also helpful to consider your view and their view on the situation and to make sure that you are not being manipulative rather than legitimately exerting your influence. What is the difference between the two? Manipulation occurs when your motives are grounded in your own purposes rather than in a common purpose (which in the work context is shared by you, the individual and the organization).

If you are motivating other people who report to other departments or organizations or who work remotely, then it is paramount that your relationship with them is one where all parties want to keep in touch. One way of developing relationships is to show a greater awareness and sensitivity to their wellbeing and work situation rather than simply being work/task-focused.

Another approach is to be useful to them – for example, as a source of knowledge or as a useful sounding board for working out problems or exploring ideas.

One common characteristic found in most people is the desire for recognition, which will be addressed in detail on Friday. While praise is assumed to be the most popular method of recognition, the ability to be genuinely interested in, and concerned about, other people is something that will inform your thinking as well as help your relationships to develop.

An additional benefit is that, through others trusting and respecting you more, they are likely to want to keep you informed and take you into their confidence. All of these methods will help you to gain a wider appreciation of situations and be able to influence decisions.

Let's look at an extended case study on influencing.

Case study: influencing

Two contemporaries, Megan and Deirdre, had begun working at Rusty Clothes Peg, the global retro female clothing brand, at the same time. After completing the graduate training scheme, Megan moved back to the United States to be based at the clothing design centre in San Francisco, while Deirdre started in the European 'satellite' office in Dublin where she worked on the European clothing range, specializing in sourcing accessories for Europe.

In Dublin, Deirdre soon became involved in liaising with a number of accessory suppliers in Asia. Her natural curiosity, patience and attention to detail meant that the suppliers liked working with her, and it made her popular. This popularity did not seem to reduce even when the pressures of seasonal launches were at their peak. While Deirdre knew she was detail-focused and placed a lot of importance on her performance, she was naturally competitive. From a young age she had learned the importance of teamwork and team spirit while competing at hockey at county level. She had progressed to the position of captain in the hockey team and was proud of this achievement.

Megan, her friend in the States, loved fashion and liked to be seen as a trendsetter rather than fashion follower. Like Deirdre, she had learned about competition from a young age when she rode in various pony trials and show-jumping competitions. Now at work in San Francisco, she had to liaise with the manufacturers in Asia and South America. Her approach was sometimes brusque and direct, and she was seen by them as an intense and highly focused individual.

Although both Megan and Deirdre were valued by the organization, the Chief Operating Officer, Glen, was fascinated to discover during a tour of the main suppliers in Asia that there was a distinct preference for dealing with the European office over the US office. Upon exploring this in more detail, Glen soon learned that the major factor was that Deirdre in Dublin had established a level of rapport with suppliers, whereas Megan in San Francisco had not. Specifically, Deirdre talked *with* people and made them feel involved, whereas Megan tended to talk *at* them.

Inside the organization, the Chief Operating Officer had recently been in a talent review meeting where Megan had been considered to be a decisive person and proactive. Indeed, she had a reputation with the senior team inside the business as a solid person you could rely on for quick action. By contrast, others thought that Deirdre was somewhat tentative at times. This seemed odd because a couple of major clients had made positive comments about Deirdre.

Below are summaries of the Chief Operating Officer's observations about the two employees, after he had gained some feedback on both individuals from their manager, peers and team members, together with his conclusions.

How Megan is seen by others

By having a positive outlook and not restricting her presence to her own department, Megan puts herself in the position where she makes sure that others learn of her success. Megan seems to have fallen into the trap of thinking that, by saying 'Fantastic', 'Well done' or 'Great job', she is recognizing other people's efforts in a positive way. However, this can be viewed as insincere at times. She has demonstrated a focus on delivering results, so that more challenging and prestigious projects are being considered for her.

How Deirdre is seen by others

Deirdre's ability to listen actively and interpret the non-verbal skills is superior to Megan's. She demonstrates that the empathy, interest and knowledge she has gleaned about other people's situations means that she is able to put into context why she thinks they have done a great job when giving positive feedback. However, she has not actively worked towards building a positive reputation inside the company but has focused on doing a good job.

Organizational awareness

1 Do you know what each function does in your organization?
2 Do you know how the work of each function affects the financial performance of your organization?

If the answer to either of those questions is 'no' then ask yourself: 'How can I find out?'

Below is a case study that is a good example of how organizational awareness can have an impact on your work.

Case study: organizational awareness

Marcus was a very confident character who was always very positive and a quick thinker. Some people described him as a 'good talker' as someone 'who could persuade anyone'. As a 'shooting star' in the organization's talent programme, he was asked to lead a small international project. Wanting to impress and complete the project early, he approached the Finance Manager, Alex, during his lunch break and explained what he needed for the project. He also wanted to tell Alex about the benefits that the project could bring to the organization in the second half of the year.

A few days later Marcus attended the weekly project update meeting. His manager, Paulette, told him that his project had been postponed. Marcus was dismayed: 'That can't be right. When I talked with Alex he said that what I was doing was interesting.'

At the end of the meeting Paulette asked Marcus to stay behind. When everyone else had left the meeting she asked him:

- Why did you approach Alex?
- How essential was it that you involved Alex?
- What other options did you have?
- What do you think the wider implications were?

When Marcus started to give Paulette vague long answers; she stopped him and explained that he urgently needed to pay more attention to how he was thinking and behaving. Although he was talented, his interpersonal skills were not as good as he thought. His team were becoming quite demotivated because he was not really listening to them or involving them.

She also told him that the pace at which he was driving the project meant he was placing unnecessary pressure on his team. Because it was an international project he should have used video and telephone conference calls more, and emails less. Because of his bullish approach, he had missed some obvious non-verbal signals (e.g. tone of voice and body language).

Lastly, his growing confidence had turned into arrogance in the eyes of his project team and a number of his peer group. Instead of using the incredible network he had at his disposal through the 'shooting star' talent programme, he had ignored this route, which could have helped him to understand what the real impact of his project could be and to work out who his allies were.

Paulette suggested that Alex should have spoken with some of the other departments and introduced himself, outlined the project, and explained how he valued their input. The simple gesture of reaching across borders would have had a tremendously positive effect on the people he interacted with.

In closing the conversation, Paulette offered Marcus the following comments about being more organizationally aware. Before approaching people outside of his normal day-to-day work, he should:

- take the time to understand his work in the wider context of the whole organization

- know who the real influencers are and importantly how well aligned they are to the organizational core values

- consider whether his timing is right – so, with very senior people, he should check with someone in his network who either knows them or can find out whether your approach will be well received.

Paulette also explained that, after Marcus spoke to Alex and outlined his concerns, Alex passed this information on to the Financial Director. She then mentioned the project to the Chief Financial Officer, who had already had concerns about Marcus's readiness for the talent programme. It was therefore decided that, as the organization needed the project to succeed, and as it did not absolutely have to be done this financial year, the CFO had postponed it for now.

It was a salutary lesson for Marcus that he needed to develop more organizational awareness.

Inform your thinking

In what ways do you keep yourself up to date on what's going on in your organization? Some people are naturally conservative or work in highly prescriptive roles or organizations, so they may not seek a wider perspective in order to stimulate their thinking.

In a similar vein, how does your thinking inform your ideas? A manager or leader is often expected to come up with ideas to help solve problems or move solutions forward, so it is worth considering how you can stimulate your thinking and problem-solving skills.

A common phrase used for innovative thinking is 'thinking outside the box'. Peter Drucker, in his book *Innovation and Entrepreneurship,* wrote about seven 'sources of innovation'. The first three sources occur within an organization and the remaining four sources involve changes outside the organization:

● **Inside the organization**
  - Unexpected successes and unexpected failures
  - Process needs
  - Incongruities

- **Outside the organization**
  - Changes in industry and market structure
  - Changes in demographics
  - Changes in meaning and perception
  - New knowledge

Expanding upon his model, Drucker proposed that systematic innovation means monitoring the seven sources regularly as they can provide opportunities for innovation. Often, the lines between these seven sources can be fuzzy and overlap. You should try, however, to treat each area separately as this will produce a better result.

The unexpected

No matter whether the unexpected is a success, a failure or an external event (within the organization or team you are in), consider whether any part of your work or the organization can benefit. If there is something, then ask (as appropriate):

1 How did the unexpected success/failure happen?
2 What would it mean to the organization if it were able to exploit the unexpected success?
3 What would have to be done to convert the unexpected failure into an opportunity?

Set aside time to discuss unexpected success or failures – they can lead to an improvement and a source of fresh motivation.

Process needs

These relate to process improvement through innovation. An example of this is where technology has been used to streamline a process, as in airlines that have developed the concept of using only online check-in for flights. As a result, they have saved time and money, as the check-in activity is carried out by the customer, not a member of staff.

Incongruities

Be vigilant for incongruity – this is the discrepancy that lies between reality as it 'actually is' and reality as it 'is assumed to be' or as it 'ought to be'. A good way to discover incongruities is to listen out for complaints or extreme views that don't seem quite right to you. Your sense of incongruity will help you to be curious about and explore what lies beneath what you have heard. For example, you might hear one department member complaining about a member of another department: 'We all work for one organization, yet despite our requests they keep not giving us the information we need.' This type of comment may indicate that the values or priorities in each department are different and can provide an opportunity to explore what could be done differently so that the information required is transferred correctly and on time. This will help future communication to be more effective and can lead to greater success.

Changes in industry and market structure

This relates to a change in a market such as the introduction of low-cost airlines into the travel industry. This changed the travelling habits of the general public. Similarly, when an industry grows very fast and demand outstrips supply, the changes and opportunities that arise can lead to innovation.

Demographics

Typically, this refers to population changes such as changes in size, age profile, educational status and income. For example, when a new shopping mall, distribution centre or major employer moves in, or out, of an area, things will change. (Note: although classed as external, this opportunity can occur when organizations are merged.)

Changes in meaning and perception

An example of this source of innovation is how business opportunities continue to develop as we continue to live longer and remain healthy and active for longer. This has created a range of opportunities – in everything from travel, hobbies and fashion to financial planning – as well as a mood of greater opportunity and enjoyment in retirement.

New knowledge

It is said in some quarters that we have moved from the Information Age to the Hybrid Age, though others have called it the Connected Age. What is certain is that, if we don't keep pace with all the new knowledge, then individuals and organizations fall behind very quickly. Therefore having areas of specialism and working collaboratively is for many organizations the only way to keep up with the rapidly changing opportunities that technology and innovation are providing. That, of course, is impossible for all but bionic brains, but we can stay informed in our respective areas of endeavours, and get together with associates and friends from differing backgrounds in order to exchange ideas.

Keep yourself informed

As a manager or leader, you would not want to be thought of as myopic or negative, so having a broad range of knowledge and social awareness as well as a positive outlook will make you more interesting and informed. This can help you to anticipate issues, be an 'out-of-the-box' thinker and, ultimately, be a source of inspirational thinking that others will want to access.

Solution support

- How often do you seek support from others – regularly, occasionally or only when you need to?
- What causes you to seek support? A problem you cannot solve or the desire to improve?
- Whom do you go to for support? The same 'comfortable' group of people, or do you challenge yourself and ask people who you know have the knowledge but might be more difficult to deal with?

If you don't seek support when trying to solve problems or at least check that who you ask for advice is worthy of providing it, how do you know you have found a good solution?

When you are managing or leading others, it is important to involve them when generating new ideas or options that could bring about changes or improvements. Sometimes we make excuses that there is not enough time and we prefer to solve our problems on our own, but if you are able to work with, and learn from, others who think and behave quite differently from you, then it can generate new ideas and approaches.

Teamwork can be frenetic, competitive and complex, and can be highly results-focused. However, given good team spirit and a willingness to engage in debate and even face disagreement, the personal benefits can outweigh working in isolation.

Obviously, working in a team is not the only way to gain support from others; specialists can offer valuable knowledge and experience, as can confidants. As you develop in an organization, the ability to get inspiration and ideas from other people is vital. This can help to improve your performance and, ultimately, also the performance of those whom you manage and lead.

Summary

Today you will have learned more about taking in the wider perspective and how it can help you motivate others. Being able to step out from within ourselves to consider the wider environment will add richness to the way that we and our teams operate.

If you want to help motivate or inspire others, then being a positive influence needs to be fundamental to your approach and requires you to be positive in your thoughts as well as actions. When working in multi-departmental teams or groups, try to be inclusive and open-minded, as these are attributes that will help to endear you to others and encourage them to be influenced by you.

When your behaviour is observed by other departments or organizations, they make judgements about your ability, and being able to take note of their different perspectives can be helpful when navigating your way in an organization.

Finally, bear in mind that the impressions you transmit as well as those you receive are vital motivational influencers.

Fact-check (answers at the back)

1. Which of the following is *not* part of Adair's Action-Centred Leadership model?
   a) Sense of identity ☐
   b) Sense of purpose ☐
   c) Sense of direction ☐
   d) Sense of belonging ☐

2. Activities that can help you in 'achieving the task' can include:
   a) Standards ☐
   b) Briefing ☐
   c) Team spirit ☐
   d) Clarifying the purpose ☐

3. Activities that can help you to build and maintain a team are:
   a) Supporting others ☐
   b) Recognition ☐
   c) Targets ☐
   d) Progress ☐

4. 'Developing the individual' can involve:
   a) Targets ☐
   b) Briefing ☐
   c) Training ☐
   d) Team spirit ☐

5. John Adair's 50/50 Rule refers to the fact that:
   a) 50 per cent of your problems come from 50 per cent of your team ☐
   b) There's a 50:50 chance that you will work with motivated people in your team ☐
   c) Praise and recognition will increase motivation by 50 per cent ☐
   d) 50 per cent of motivation comes from within a person and 50 per cent from his or her environment, especially from the leadership encountered there ☐

6. Developing organizational awareness is:
   a) Managing your boss more effectively ☐
   b) About getting a better job ☐
   c) Finding out about companies that are similar to the one you work in ☐
   d) Understanding how other departments in the organization operate ☐

7. When leaders have a sound understanding of how the business and organization around them works:
a) They know how to find the expertise they require, where to find it and how to access it ❏
b) They know which boss is difficult to work with ❏
c) They have been distracted from the job of getting on with the real work ❏
d) They know how to work the system ❏

8. Which one of the following does not feature among Drucker's seven sources of innovation?
a) New knowledge ❏
b) The 50/50 Rule ❏
c) Changes in demographics ❏
d) Unexpected successes or failures ❏

9. When you are looking to generate new ideas or innovative ways of solving a problem, it is useful to:
a) Ask people who have the knowledge but might be more difficult to deal with ❏
b) Just save time and try to fix the problem yourself ❏
c) Speak to the same people you always speak to ❏
d) Ask your manager ❏

10. Which activity below has potentially a long-lasting negative impact?
a) Trying to fix all your problems on your own without asking for help ❏
b) Speaking to your boss's boss without checking that it is OK first ❏
c) Scowling at or showing no interest in someone the first time you meet them ❏
d) Working collaboratively with your peers at work ❏

THURSDAY

Dealing with difficult situations

We are now over halfway through the week and you should have gained a greater understanding of the key elements that influence motivation, as well as of some of the actions you can take, as a manager, to inspire and motivate other people.

You will also now realize how important it is to create the right environment so that people can perform at their best, while enabling them to have a degree of autonomy in their work. If these things, along with your encouragement and direction, are in place, you are likely to have happier and more engaged people in your team.

However, it is also likely that there will be times when the motivation level of individuals in your team can dip. This can be because of external factors such as the economy, or changes in their personal circumstances such as marriage breakdown or family tensions. It can also be due to issues within your organization such as unsettling internal politics, difficult colleagues or unrealistic time pressures.

Today we will focus on some of the common problems that cause people to become demotivated, and how to address them as a manager.

Managing internal politics

Case study: the dangers of ignoring internal politics

Jorgen had been working on a report for a week. Along with his team, he had done a great job in analysing and collating all the data required to prove the need for an additional member of staff to work in the accounting function. He was confident that when he presented the arguments to Katarina, the company director, she would agree to what was proposed. After all, everyone had seemed enthusiastic about the idea at the monthly meeting.

When Jorgen presented the proposal to Katarina, she thanked him, and said she would let him know what the decision was. After a few days, she told him that the proposal had been rejected because another manager had made a stronger case, and so they would get the additional resourcing. Jorgen was furious. It had all seemed so straightforward – so something must have changed.

What Jorgen was not aware of was that the other manager had been subtly influencing Katarina for some time, so that by the time Jorgen submitted his proposal the other manager had succeeded in winning over Katarina. Jorgen had been beaten by internal politics.

It is important, particularly within large organizations, to understand how the internal politics operate, because those who have power and influence are likely to have an impact on your ability to get things done. You don't have to like everyone you work with, but you have to be able to get on with them. Make sure that you develop good peer relationships so that you know what's going on.

There can be a dark side to organizational politics – people behave in a selfish manner, have personal conflicts, compete for power and leadership, and use influence to build personal status by controlling access to information or not revealing the true intent behind their behaviour. Some people avoid 'playing the game' because they don't like this type of behaviour and therefore miss out on the positive benefits that can be gained by having informal networks and being able to assert their presence in an authentic and positive way.

Think back to the key points about what motivates people to take action:

● the strength of their needs
● their perception that taking an action will satisfy those needs.

If you perceive that investing time in building relationships and getting to know key people will not bring you any benefit, then it is unlikely that you will be motivated to spend time on this activity. However, if you consider this in a different way, and ask yourself the question 'How will building relationships with key people help my team to get their work done more effectively?', you might come up with a different response. It is likely that the quality of relationships and breadth of the network you create will have a degree of influence over how peers respond to requests from you or your team members.

Case study: learning how to influence

Henri was an up-and-coming manager in a biotechnology company. He wanted to be able to influence the Chief Scientific Officer (CSO) more effectively, but found it difficult to speak to him in team meetings, and, as a result, his ideas and concerns were getting ignored. The CSO had a very direct style and did not suffer fools gladly. Every time Henri asked a challenging question, the CSO seemed to respond abruptly and glare at him.

Frustrated at his lack of progress, Henri confided in his colleague Arianna, who was also a manager. He explained his issue and asked for her thoughts. 'Have you ever paid attention to how other people influence the CSO?' she replied. 'They make sure they catch him at the water cooler, and strike up a conversation with him about his passion, which is golf. Then they move the discussion on to whatever is concerning them and see what he thinks. In this way, if there is a disagreement, it is done informally and never in the team meeting. I think that your challenging questions in the meeting put him on the spot and so he gets defensive.' Henri had never considered this before. He thanked Arianne and reflected on how he could influence the CSO in a different manner.

By taking time to stop and observe what was happening, and asking a colleague for advice, he was able to understand the subtle politics that were at play and how others got things done. This enabled him to adopt an approach that still felt authentic, but helped him to avoid confronting the CSO in public, which was not delivering the result he wanted.

Motive for action = To get the CSO to buy in to Henri's ideas

Behaviour = Asking peers what their observations were

Result = Understanding the politics helped to create more options for different approaches Henri could take

Additional benefit = Less frustration for Henri and a stronger relationship with his colleague Arianna

External influences

As a manager, it is essential that you also pay attention to anything going on in the wider world that could have an impact on the behaviour and motivation levels of people in the workplace. For example, the global financial crisis made its mark on many people financially through job losses or reduced work hours, organizational cost cutting, the suspension or cancelling of projects, and so on. There was a change from a period of high confidence to one of uncertainty, anxiety and concern. Coping with uncertain times meant that employees tended to focus on their own financial security, family obligations and future employment prospects (remember the first and second level of Maslow's Hierarchy of Needs).

This uncertainty can escalate into rumour and gossip and before long people feel disinclined to perform at their best.

There are a number of ways in which you can support your team in managing their distress and anxiety. Communication is a key element here:

- Don't ignore reality. If there are external issues that are causing concern, recognize this and talk about them openly with your team.
- Use a variety of methods to communicate with your team so as to ensure that they are aware.
- Check that they have understood what you have communicated.
- Find out what the rumours and gossip are so that you are 'in the loop'.
- Take time to listen to the concerns of your staff but don't get bogged down in the uncertainty yourself.
- Encourage people to focus on the aspects of the situation that they can control, and to stop worrying about what is beyond their control.
- Every challenge can also be an opportunity, so think about what the opportunity could be.
- Turn the focus back on to what still has to be achieved despite any uncertainty. Satisfaction can still be gained from achieving results.

 Get great results in times of uncertainty
Great results can still be achieved in times of disruption and uncertainty if a team focuses on what they can change, rather than on what they cannot change. As a manager, you can empathize but do not join the team in feeling disempowered or ineffective. Make sure that you are aware of your own emotions, because they can have an impact on your behaviour and your team will notice your own feelings of uncertainty or negativity.

Unrealistic timescales

Another external influence that can either inspire or demotivate people is being given a task that has an unrealistic timescale in which to achieve it. Most people have experienced this at some stage in their working lives, when they find that they are asked to complete a job in a time that they believe is impossible.

Case study: giving people a choice

Dean was a graphic designer in a design and print company. Their client suddenly changed the design of the invitations for an event the evening before they were due to be printed and sent out. Normally, Dean finished work at 17:30, and when his manager asked him to revise the design at 17:00 he knew that the timescale was unrealistic.

Dean's manager explained the reason for the change and how important this client was to their overall business. He added: 'I know I don't normally ask you to work late, but on this occasion, if you are able to, you would be helping out not just me and the client, but the entire company. I would really appreciate it if you are able to help.'

This gave Dean an element of control and choice in his decision, and although he knew there was not really any choice in reality, he appreciated that his manager had spoken to him in this way, rather than just telling him to stay late and get on with it. By giving Dean a choice, his manager was using the Self-Determination Theory we looked at on Tuesday, and as a result Dean was willing to stay late.

The other approach that Dean's manager could have taken was one of coercion and command. An American social psychologist, Douglas McGregor, describes this type of strategy as typical of a Theory X manager. McGregor's ideas suggested that there are two fundamental approaches to managing people. Many managers tend towards Theory X and generally get poor results.

Enlightened managers use Theory Y, which is similar to how Dean's manager behaved, which can produce better performance and results, and allows people to grow and develop.

Contrasting beliefs of Theory X and Theory Y managers

Beliefs of Theory X manager (authoritarian management style)	Beliefs of Theory Y manager (participative management style)
The average person dislikes work and will avoid it if they can.	The effort people put in at work is as natural as work and play.
Most people must be forced with the threat of punishment to work towards organizational objectives.	People will apply self-control and self-direction in the pursuit of organizational objectives, without external control or the threat of punishment.
The average person prefers to be directed, to avoid responsibility, is relatively unambitious, and wants security above all else.	People usually accept and often seek responsibility.
	Commitment to objectives is a function of the rewards associated with their achievement.
	The capacity to use a high degree of imagination, ingenuity and creativity in solving organizational problems is widely, not narrowly, distributed in the population. In industry, the intellectual potential of the average person is only partly utilized.

If Dean's manager had been a Theory X manager, it is likely that his approach with Dean would have been quite different – he would have just told him that they needed the revised invitation by 19:00 that night and to get it done. This is because Theory X managers tend to be results-oriented and focused on the facts and figures, and don't understand, or have any interest, in the 'people' issues.

If you have to work with a Theory X manager, it is useful to have some knowledge of how to work with them effectively – and thereby influence them.

Things to know about Theory X managers

● **They are results-oriented** – so focus your own discussions and dealings with them around results, on what you can deliver and when. Focus and get agreement on the results and deadlines – if you deliver consistently, you'll increasingly be given more leeway on how you go about the tasks, which amounts to more freedom.
● **They are focused on facts and figures** – so cut out the incidental information and be able to measure and

substantiate anything you say and do for them, especially when reporting on results and activities.

- **They do not understand or have an interest in people issues** – so don't try to appeal to their sense of humanity. Set your own objectives to meet their organizational aims and agree these with them. Show them that you are self-motivating, self-disciplined and well organized.

Ways to deal with Theory X managers

- **Always deliver on your commitments and promises.** If you are given an unrealistic task and/or deadline, state the reason why it is not realistic but be very sure of your ground. Try to be constructive as to how the overall aim can be achieved in a way that you know you can deliver.
- **Stand up for yourself but avoid confrontation.** Never threaten to go over their heads if you are dissatisfied. If you do, you'll be in big trouble afterwards and life will be a lot more difficult.
- **Don't add to their problems.** Be aware that many managers are forced to adopt a Theory X approach by the short-term demands of the organization and their own superiors. A Theory X manager is usually someone with their own problems, so try not to give them any more.

Dealing with underperformers

Another challenge that you may face as a manager is finding a way to deal with underperformers. Failure to do so can lead to an entire team becoming discontent. If a manager continually avoids addressing the issue, it can ultimately be the manager who is managed out of the organization! Use the following strategy:

1 Find out the reason

Make sure that you do not make assumptions about what is causing the poor performance. Reasons can vary from lack of skill and clear goals, to lack of interest and focus due to personal issues outside work. Is it just this one person in one situation?

Has it developed over a period of time? How do you know they are not performing – what is the measure you are using?

Sometimes underperformance can be due to poor management, because no overall goals or objectives have been jointly set, so be prepared to look at your own practices as a manager before jumping to conclusions.

2 Take action

The longer that a person is left to underperform, the greater effect their underperformance is likely to have on the overall team – morale and productivity will slip as others see that the issue is not being addressed. So take action by having a discussion with the person and allowing them time to improve their performance. Make sure that you both have clarity about what level of performance is expected, and what changes in behaviour you wish to observe, and by when. Explain the consequences if the behaviour does not improve within the agreed timescales.

3 Consider the wider consequences

The way that a manager handles underperformance will be noticed by others in the organization. If people see that managers give underperformers a chance to improve, and support to do so, and that there are consequences if they do not do so, they will understand better what the likely implications for them could be if they did not deliver results. However, if a team notices that the manager fails to tackle poor performance, or that there is an overall absence of clear goals and expectations of what should be achieved, they are more likely to be apathetic and less keen to perform well.

4 Choose the appropriate leadership style

Picking up on point 2, if the style that you normally adopt as a manager to motivate members of your team is not working, it may be worth while considering a different approach. A *Harvard Business Review* article by Robert Tannenbaum and Warren H.

Schmidt entitled 'How to Choose a Leadership Pattern' offers a continuum of leadership behaviour that relates the degree of authority used by a manager to the degree of freedom available to their subordinates.

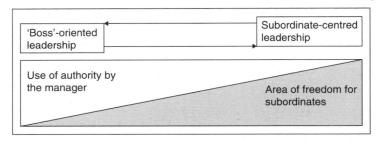

Tannenbaum and Schmidt's continuum of leadership behaviour

This continuum provides a useful reference for the different approaches you may select for making a decision, and assessing the potential consequences. At the right-hand end of the continuum subordinates enjoy a high degree of freedom. (This is similar to the degree of autonomy described in Deci's Self-Determination Theory on Tuesday, where the more autonomy that individuals have, the more their motivation will come from within.)

There are four main styles: tell, sell, consult and involve:

● The **Tell manager** will identify a problem, choose a decision or action plan and instruct the subordinates/team.
● The **Sell manager**, unlike the Tell manager, recognizes that subordinates may be resistant or have issues. So, although the Sell manager will have already come to a decision, they will attempt to persuade the subordinates to adopt the decision and action plan.
● The **Consult manager** will have views on what a decision and action plan should be but will not state those until the subordinates/team have had an opportunity to discuss the problem/task. Only after that will the Consult manager decide on the action plan, which enables individuals to feel they have had a say in the decision.

- The **Involve manager** will define the problem/task and the limits of responsibility, and will then involve the subordinates/team totally in the decision process – there will be a discussion and then the team, along with the manager, will make the decision/action plan.

This range of styles can give you a wider range of options for managing people, and it can be helpful to review which style seems to help/hinder performance with particular individuals.

Personal issues that impact on work

You already know how to create a work environment that gives employees a sense of identity, belonging and direction (see Wednesday). However, there may be situations when you notice that those you have to manage seem to be 'off their game' and it's your job to understand what is going on so that you can help them get back to being at their best.

Sometimes personal issues outside work can have an impact on their performance. For example, if a family member is ill or they have financial worries, when the person is at work they will find it difficult to concentrate. While providing support and empathy as a manager is helpful, it is also useful to make it clear to the person that you still need them to deliver results at work. At times, it may also be difficult to interpret an individual's behaviour because they may not always be willing to talk about the underlying cause.

It can be beneficial to liaise with the human resources department, which can support the employee and direct the individual to any additional resources that might be available such as employee assistance, occupational health or a stress management programme.

In addition to these unexpected personal issues, there may be other influences that a person may not be consciously aware of that causes them to behave in a manner that is out of the norm. In this case, their behaviour can be driven

Continuum of leadership behaviour: making a decision

Manager-led	Subordinate-led
Manager makes decision and announces it	Manager presents problem, receives suggestions and makes decision
Manager 'sells' decision	Manager defines the boundariesand asks individuals to make decision
Manager presents ideas and invites questions	Manager permits subordinates to function within limits defined by business or their 'boss'
Manager presents tentative decision, subject to change	

by underlying personality traits that may not be normally observable. Consider the following:

- **Their level of desire for independence** If you put a person who normally works independently into a team situation, they may find it difficult to operate.
- **Willingness to tolerate ambiguity** Some people can operate with a high degree of uncertainty whereas others prefer to minimize risks and be more in control of an outcome.
- **Knowledge and experience to deal with tasks** Some people find it hard to admit that they don't know how to do something, so, if you give them a task and assume that they know what to do, they might find it hard to tell you otherwise.
- **Willingness to share knowledge in the decision-making process** This point can be linked to the independence issue above, particularly if the organization has a culture where 'information is power'. It is likely to be difficult for a person to accept that others may have to be involved in the process of making a decision, because it could mean having to disclose information.

Summary

Today you should now have a better idea of ways to deal with problems that you may encounter as a manager when having to motivate other people. Whether it is being able to understand the politics that operate within an organization, or becoming aware of how external factors can influence how people react at work, it can be good to have a greater knowledge of what is going on, and how to navigate these situations.

As a manager, sometimes your own motivation can be tested if you are given unrealistic timescales in which to achieve particular results. The section on Theory X and Y managers will resonate with what you read earlier in the book about Self-Determination Theory and the importance of meeting underlying needs such as autonomy, competence and relatedness.

Getting to grips with underperformers may call for tough talk and straight dealing as well as empathy and understanding. Being a manager for all types of people demands the ability to adapt your style, so practise flexing your style to see how both you and other people react to different behaviours!

SUNDAY
MONDAY
TUESDAY
WEDNESDAY
THURSDAY
FRIDAY
SATURDAY

Fact-check (answers at the back)

1. Understanding organizational politics is about:
   a) Being nice to the boss ❏
   b) Knowing how informal influence is used within the organization ❏
   c) Taking a short cut on the career ladder ❏
   d) Getting ahead with your job by getting to know the CEO ❏

2. In order to gauge your manager's views on a subject that is to be discussed at a meeting, you could:
   a) Find out who your manager goes to lunch with, and ask them ❏
   b) Send your manager an email giving your views ❏
   c) Casually ask for their thoughts on the subject prior to the meeting ❏
   d) Grab them in the coffee lounge and spend ten minutes giving your point of view ❏

3. Which of the following is *not* something that will help you cope when external issues impact on your team?
   a) Recognizing when issues are causing concern, and talking about them openly with your team ❏
   b) Turning the focus back on to what still has to be achieved despite any uncertainty ❏
   c) Panicking and starting to get worried ❏
   d) Finding out what the rumours and gossip are so you are informed ❏

4. Theory X managers:
   a) Do not understand or have an interest in people issues ❏
   b) Are interested in lots of extra detail and extraneous information ❏
   c) Are focused on the big picture ❏
   d) Take time to really get to know their staff to build good relationships ❏

5. Theory Y managers:
   a) Think that the average person prefers to be directed ❏
   b) Believe that people must be forced to work towards goals by the threat of punishment ❏
   c) Believe that people are inherently lazy and not interested in work ❏
   d) Have a participative management style ❏

6. If you have a Theory X manager, you should:
   a) Threaten them, and go over their head if you are upset ❏
   b) Appeal to their sense of humanity ❏
   c) Deliver on your commitments and promises ❏
   d) Have a vague and rambling discussion with them ❏

7. Which of the following is *not* an action to take when dealing with underperformers?
   a) Find out the reason ❏
   b) Take action ❏
   c) Consider the wider consequences ❏
   d) Accept that it is just how they are ❏

8. The four different management styles discussed by Tannenbaum and Schmidt are:
a) Tell, Sell, Consult, Involve ❏
b) See, Hear, Do, Predict ❏
c) Task, Team, Individual, Purpose ❏
d) Participative, Coercive, Team-focused, Autonomous ❏

9. When individuals' personal issues impact on their work, as a manager you should:
a) Be empathetic and understanding, but clear about expectations ❏
b) Tell them to get a grip and focus on their work ❏
c) Send them to HR and avoid dealing with the issue ❏
d) Ignore them and hope that things change ❏

10. Which of the following theories of motivation highlight the issue of 'intrinsic motivation'? (There are more than one.)
a) Maslow's Hierarchy of Needs ❏
b) Herzberg's Theory of Motivation ❏
c) Deci and Ryan's Self-determination Theory ❏
d) McGregor's Theory X and Theory Y ❏

FRIDAY

Rewards and recognition

Sometimes, no matter how hard you work, you just don't get recognized. Today we focus on this subject because it is so important to motivation. We will use an extended case study to illustrate the key learning points.

We will take a look at different aspects of reward and recognition to which it is critical for you, as a manager, to pay attention. These aspects are:

- monetary rewards
- non-financial rewards
- appreciation and recognition
- incentives.

Sometimes hard work goes unnoticed...

Let's begin by introducing our case study.

> ## Case study: Llewellyn feels his extra work goes unappreciated
>
> For three weeks Llewellyn had been working late on a Friday evening and been expected to come in over the weekend to maintain the company IT system. Everyone else had gone home, and while he was waiting for an upgrade to finish he allowed his mind to drift and reflect back over the last six months. His partner, Alfredo, had recently asked him: 'Lew, why do you spend so much time at work when the company won't invest in improving the IT system? If it wasn't for your knowledge and goodwill, they would be stuck, yet they don't even pay you anything for the extra hours you work. It must be 20 hours every week and that's before you include the time you are checking things remotely from home!'
>
> It was the word 'goodwill' that Llewellyn was reflecting on. On a mental blank page he was jotting down where and when he had received any positive communication from anyone senior in the organization. It stayed blank. By contrast, he had already filled up another mental page with all the IT-related issues and problems the organization had brought to him. Eight-seven per cent of them were as a result of a policy of minimal investment in the proper upgrading of firmware, software and hardware, or providing any training for users.

Monetary rewards

'How much do you earn?' is a question you will be asked at some time in your career and it is no doubt a question you would like to ask others. As a manager or leader, it is so important to do your utmost to ensure fairness in terms of monetary rewards. This means checking that those you are responsible for are fairly paid for their job role, their level of responsibility and the performance they deliver at work.

Fairness is important, not just in your area of direct responsibility, but across other comparable roles in your organization, because it is inevitable that employees will discover what others earn. For example, if sales administration staff have higher salaries than purchasing administration, even though their jobs are similar, you can anticipate significant demotivation in the purchasing team.

Rewards aren't just a question of money
As a manager, it is also useful to be aware of the different elements that constitute rewards because money is only one element. To help you gain this wider perspective, this chapter addresses other elements of reward and recognition that play a part in having motivated employees.

Case study: Llewellyn's salary

What would have happened if the company had paid Llewellyn more in recognition of the value he delivers to the business and the unsociable extra hours he works? Were he to be paid more, do you think he would be fully satisfied?

The likelihood is that the frustration Llewellyn experienced would continue unless he developed greater job satisfaction internally, and also won appreciation or recognition from his managers. It is important not to assume that monetary rewards should be the first and only way of rewarding people, as was highlighted on Monday in the section on recognition and appreciation.

Sometimes managers operate by giving positive feedback by 'exception' and commenting only when something has gone wrong, rather than noticing what has been done well. For someone like Llewellyn, it is likely to be demotivating, as his personality preference appears to show that he is more externally referenced – he likes to know that he is doing a good job (see Sunday on Meta Programs).

Non-financial rewards

In many companies, managers have no ability to give additional financial rewards, so they have to think about how they can reward someone without increasing their earnings. Below are listed six categories of non-financial reward. This is not an exhaustive list but should provide a good basis for you to work from.

1 **Achievement or contribution** – for example publicly mentioning an individual's successes, efforts (even in failure), solutions or ideas and how they have helped
2 **Growth opportunities** – giving the individual the chance to develop their professional status or knowledge (e.g. investment in time off to take a course or academic qualification)
3 **Networking** – giving the individual the opportunity to meet and work with other people of significance from around the organization or further afield (e.g. key clients or suppliers can provide employees with great opportunities to learn skills and interpersonal relations plus extend their network)
4 **Advancement** – enabling the individual to become part of a project team, and thereby stretching their skills and developing their opportunities for advancement

5 **Leadership** – projects or initiatives can provide a great 'incubator' for people to demonstrate their leadership and management potential offline from the organization structure

6 **Environment** – upgrading an individual's tools (e.g. computer) or improving their physical working conditions

These non-monetary rewards are incorporated into the 'Total Reward' approach, as proposed by Patricia K. Zingheim and Jay R. Schuster in *Pay People Right!* This breaks down rewards into four elements, as shown below:

The components of Zingheim and Schuster's 'Total Reward'

In dividual growth	Compelling future
Investment in employees	Compelling vision
Development and training	Company growth and success
Opportunity to be multi-skilled and take on different roles	Company image and reputation Win-win over time
Total pay	**Positive work environment**
Base pay	Inspiring leadership
Variable pay (e.g. bonus)	Operating infrastructure
Share options for key people	Colleagues
Benefits (e.g. coffee, holidays)	Work itself
Recognition	Effective relationships

These components enable an individual to understand the broader perspective when it comes to thinking about how they are rewarded. Often, employees compare their current situation to others, only by using salary as the benchmark, but the truth is that rewards are made up of far more than money. If an employee is helped to look at the other elements of reward, they can begin to judge their situation in a different way. For example, the fact that an organization has a strong brand reputation and a clear vision for where the business is heading will influence how employees feel about working there.

So encourage those you have to motivate to consider the wider view of rewards rather than just their salary.

Appreciation and recognition

All too often, appreciation or recognition is assumed but not expressed. Many organizations are managed on a problem-solving basis, which means that a lot of energy is expended on anticipating, identifying, monitoring and solving problems. Proportionally, a lot less energy is used in appreciating the efforts and performance of its people. On Monday, we explained the difference between appreciation and recognition and the suitability of each for motivating different members of your team.

We have also highlighted that the amount of power and influence you can wield through exhibiting positive energy is quite remarkable, especially when it is delivered face to face and on a one-to-one basis. What can make a demonstration of appreciation even more powerful is when you put that appreciation into context.

Acknowledging someone's effort in working late by saying 'Thank you' is good if you can show that:

● you understand what was required from them in order to do it
● you understand what their effort and/or result means to the organization
● you are genuinely thinking about them and their needs.

For example, according to the Myers-Briggs Type Indicator, someone with a Thinking preference is likely to be prefer recognition from someone significant in the organization whom they respect, and they also might want to be given more work as a reward. By contrast, those with a Feeling preference are more likely to appreciate receiving a handwritten thank-you card or box of chocolates that has been selected specially for them. It is not the monetary value that is the issue, but the personal consideration that has been shown to them.

Get to know your team
By getting to know more about the people you have to manage, you can learn about their interests outside work and which gifts would mean the most to them. The choice of gift will be a good indicator to the recipient of your true appreciation.

'If then' or 'now that' rewards

It is important not to express your intention of giving a gift until the work is complete. To mention a gift beforehand could have the effect of being an incentive rather than the genuine sign of appreciation that you intend. Daniel Pink, in *Drive: The Surprising Truth about What Motivates Us*, describes this difference as that between 'if then' and 'now that' rewards.

'Now that' is used after the event as a method of recognition – for example, 'Now that you have worked extra hours over the weekend to help sort out the IT system, I'd like to give you a day off in lieu of the hours worked.' This reward is unexpected and does not set up the employee to expect this to happen all the time.

'If then' is used as an incentive or form of extrinsic motivation before the action is taken – for example, 'If you come in over the weekend and help out, then you can have an extra day off.' The downside of this approach is that it can reduce an individual's intrinsic motivation (see Herzberg's theory of motivation, discussed on Sunday). This sets up an expectation in the person's mind that, the next time they are asked to help out, they can expect a similar reward. So it can actually achieve the opposite effect for the organization in the longer term, as it encourages employees to do extra work only when there is some sort of reward for doing so.

> ## Case study: showing Llewellyn appreciation
>
> From the case study it would seem that Llewellyn was not given even the most basic appreciation. His manager could have said 'thank you' or made an occasional phone call when he was working late to find out how he was getting on. Expressing appreciation for his efforts could have changed the level of motivation that Llewellyn had for doing the work.

What else would you suggest could be done in terms of recognizing Llewellyn's efforts?

Incentives

Commonly, the reason for introducing an incentive is to encourage your team members to put in a greater effort. Being clear about what incentivizing means to you is extremely beneficial because, if you aren't, incentive programmes can end up not having the desired effect. It is also worth while understanding how those you have to manage like to be incentivized, too.

When considering the use of an incentive, it is important to ask yourself whether the incentive you are thinking of using is one that appeals to the values and needs of all concerned (i.e. you, the organization and the individuals to be incentivized). Do not fall into the trap of making assumptions about this because what works for you is not necessarily likely to work for everyone else.

Also, you should decide on the level of performance you are seeking through the incentive. If the change you are expecting to get is a permanent or major one, then will the incentive remain valid and sustainable throughout? It may be that the extra motivation you think will be gained by offering a 'carrot' at the end is not continued over time because intrinsic motivation is reduced (see Daniel Pink's 'if then' approach above).

For example, If Llewellyn's manager had offered him a bonus for working over the weekend, it might do the trick on the first occasion. However, if he is required to continue working at weekends, Llewellyn is likely to expect a bonus every time, and if this is not forthcoming, then he is likely to become even more demotivated than he was before being offered the incentive.

Incentives encourage people to be forward thinking – but at what cost? If the incentive period is short, then will any sacrifices of behaviour, practices and values be made in order to achieve the incentive?

There is also the risk with incentives that they are too materially oriented and become the norm. If an incentive becomes the assumed expectation (i.e. the reason for doing something), then the likelihood is that the motivational driver is no longer about core values and the organizational mission – it is about personal gain. A likely consequence is that incentives devalue appreciation and a 'thank you' becomes ineffective.

Finally, when considering using incentives, make sure they are part of an integrated approach that supports the organization and complements any reward programme. The context of the incentive is something worth spending time explaining when launching and reinforcing its purpose during the period that it is in place.

Case study: benefits for Llewellyn and the organization

Given the way in which Llewellyn applied himself, it would seem that his work ethic is very strong, so would more appreciation and recognition of his efforts and performance be more effective for him and the organization?

In future, make sure your recognition is:

- **timely** – try to catch people doing something right
- **authentic** – make sure that you really mean what you say (don't just thoughtlessly say 'Great job!')
- **in context** – relevant to the scale of the achievement
- **linked to the person's own values, and not your own** – step into their shoes and make the reward meaningful to them.

Summary

Today you have assembled a number of strategies and techniques for demonstrating your appreciation and recognition of others for their effort and performance. Equally, you will now have spent time thinking about how, why and when you might use incentives and rewards to help motivate and focus people on issues important to you and the organization.

While commonly people associate the term 'reward' with money, you will now have ideas for alternative, non-monetary rewards. How a person's role is structured, their autonomy and the support they receive, along with the degree to which they are interested and stimulated by the role and work content, will all influence the degree to which they are motivated. It does not take much for people to become demotivated when managers are not fully attentive to the non-verbal signals people display.

Tomorrow you can re-evaluate your strategy for strengthening how you motivate yourself and how you can help to motivate and inspire others.

SUNDAY

MONDAY

TUESDAY

WEDNESDAY

THURSDAY

FRIDAY

SATURDAY

Fact-check (answers at the back)

1. Which of the following forms of reward and recognition tend to reduce intrinsic motivation?
   a) Monetary rewards ❏
   b) Non-monetary rewards ❏
   c) Appreciation and recognition ❏
   d) Incentives ❏

2. Financial rewards in a team should be based on:
   a) Fairness and parity ❏
   b) Giving the most to those who do the most work ❏
   c) Years of service ❏
   d) Ability to do the job ❏

3. You can reward someone while not directly increasing their earnings by:
   a) Encouraging them to work longer hours ❏
   b) Providing opportunities for training and development ❏
   c) Moving them to a new location ❏
   d) Highlighting their individual successes ❏

4. Which of the elements below is *not* part of Zingheim and Schuster's 'Total Reward' approach?
   a) Individual growth ❏
   b) Compelling future ❏
   c) Positive work environment ❏
   d) Bonus and incentives ❏

5. Methods of appreciation do *not* include:
   a) Giving a bonus ❏
   b) Saying 'Thank you' ❏
   c) Giving a personalized gift or token ❏
   d) Thanking an individual in front of others ❏

6. Acknowledging someone's effort can be good if you can show that you understood:
   a) What was required from them in order to do it ❏
   b) How it benefits you ❏
   c) How much they will be paid ❏
   d) Why other team members did not step up and help out ❏

7. Daniel Pink's 'now that' approach is used:
   a) As a way of showing off and bragging to your colleagues ❏
   b) Like a carrot to incentivize activity ❏
   c) After the event as a method of recognition ❏
   d) To tap into extrinsic motivation ❏

8. Daniel Pink's 'if then' approach is used:
   a) To reward success after an individual has done over and above what was expected ❏
   b) To get people to do things they don't want to do ❏
   c) After the event as a form of recognition ❏
   d) As an incentive and form of extrinsic motivation ❏

9. One of the main risks of using incentives is that:
a) They encourage long-term behaviour change ❏
b) They are too materially focused and become the norm ❏
c) They don't deliver the desired outcome ❏
d) People are so enthusiastic that it costs the company a lot of money ❏

10. Which of the following should recognition *not* necessarily be?
a) Timely ❏
b) Authentic ❏
c) Linked to the person's values ❏
d) A rare occurrence ❏

SUNDAY MONDAY TUESDAY WEDNESDAY THURSDAY FRIDAY SATURDAY

SATURDAY

Reviewing progress

As it is now the end of the week, it is time to draw together what you have read, learned and remembered from your previous experiences, and then think about how you will review the progress you have made in motivating others. In today's chapter we will consider three areas:

1 What you have learned
2 How you can review the progress of those you are trying to motivate and inspire
3 How you can encourage those you have to motivate to review their own progress.

You will also be able to explore ways in which you can prepare, conduct and learn from the reviews you do to help others develop their motivation.

In particular, today we will explore how reviewing can influence motivation, as well as how language influences what is reviewed and how reviewing is carried out. In addition, there are some monitoring tools that can be used to assess progress.

Measurement is a key part of the process of motivation because the mere activity of measuring progress can act as a motive for continuing action. For example, if you are trying to lose weight, by stepping on the scales once a week you get a measure of progress. The information you get will potentially motivate you to continue because the measure shows you are losing weight, will serve to motivate you to do better if you are not losing weight, or will cause you to give up if the goal is perceived as being too difficult to achieve. Whatever the result, without the existence of a monitoring process you do not know whether you are moving towards or away from your goal.

Context: your progress/ performance

If you are responsible for motivating others to achieve certain results, part of your strategy should be putting in place a monitoring process. This could be a daily, weekly or monthly meeting, or an update via text message or an emailed report.

Before conducting a progress review on a face-to-face basis, especially one regarding personal issues such as motivation and performance, it is important for the reviewer to be clear about how their own performance may have had some influence on the outcome so far.

So, before discussing the preparation, structure and methods of the review process, it is useful to revisit the principles behind motivation and influencing, as these will provide valuable reminders of how to put yourself 'into the shoes' of another person so that you communicate with them effectively.

Remember: people are generally motivated by their desire to satisfy a hierarchy of needs (Maslow):

- **Physiological** – hunger, thirst, sleep
- **Safety** – security, protection from danger
- **Social** – belonging, acceptance, social life, friendship and love
- **Esteem** – self-respect, achievement, status, recognition
- **Self-actualization** – growth, accomplishment, personal development

Each person you have to motivate is not necessarily focused on fulfilling the same needs, and so may need to be motivated in a different way. If a person is seeking to have their esteem needs met, it is likely that they are more interested in measuring success and receiving positive feedback, and may find it hard to be challenged or receive critical feedback that could detract from their own positive self-perception.

Reviewing intrinsic motivation

On Tuesday you read about Ryan and Deci's Self-determination Theory, where a critical distinction is made between intrinsic and extrinsic motivation.

- **Intrinsically motivated behaviours** are performed out of personal interest and personal desire – they satisfy our innate psychological needs for competence and autonomy (i.e. they form the basis for self-determined behaviour).
- **Extrinsically motivated behaviours** derive from the 'carrot and stick' approach, which is underpinned by the belief that someone would not want to do something unless there was a reward at the end (e.g. a bonus or avoiding being berated by the manager). Such behaviours are based on threat, enticement or coercion.

A tool that can help people to review their intrinsic motivation is to encourage them to ask 'active questions'. According to Marshall Goldsmith, people who ask themselves active questions on a regular basis have reported more happiness, more meaning in their lives, and better relationships. Here are some active questions you should be asking yourself regularly:

- 'What did I do to make sure I knew what was expected of me at work?'
- 'Did I do my best to progress towards my goals today?'
- 'Did I do my best to be engaged?'

The principle of active questions gets away from the passive approach in which employees can get into 'victim' mode and avoid action because they think that the organization is responsible for doing something – not them. The use of active questions enables employees to take more initiative and become more autonomous. With that greater sense of control comes greater satisfaction at work.

It is worth while remembering that there may be some generational differences related to this (we outlined these on Monday). For example, the high degree of self-reliance characterized by Generation X means that they are more likely to be proactive and take action themselves to solve problems and get the job done. Millennials, by contrast, are more likely to sit back and expect the 'organization' to provide. The use of active questions as a form of review can help people to avoid passive behaviour.

You can also use active questions to assess your own level of leadership. The table below draws on the five characteristics of exemplary leadership as identified by Jim Kouzes and Barry Posner, in *The Leadership Challenge: How to Make Extraordinary Things Happen in Organizations*. As you work through the questions, note down any reflections as these can become your personal development plan and source of self-motivation.

Reviewing your level of influence

Influencing has been a common theme throughout this week and so, in discussing the topic of reviewing progress, it is worth mentioning the Influence Model, as proposed by Allen R. Cohen and David L. Bradford. The model is based on the Law of Reciprocity, which states that all transmissions of energy result in a return of energy in a similar way. This belief is sometimes summarized as 'What you put out you get back', which is a point well worth remembering – and not just when conducting a review!

The Influence Model has six fundamental steps:

1 Assume that the person you are attempting to influence is your ally.
2 Clarify your goals and priorities.
3 Think about the other person and their world view, vision and values.

4 Identify relevant 'currencies' – what matters to you and the other person.
5 Understand and deal with your relationship with that person.
6 Influence the person through give and take.

You can use these steps as a checklist for your behaviour when trying to motivate other people, by asking yourself: 'Did I do my best to 1) assume that the other person was my ally... 2) clarify my goals and priorities...?' and so on.

Kouzes and Posner's five practices of exemplary leadership

Did you do your best to...		
... model the way?	• Set the example • Plan small wins	Leaders, through their own leadership behaviour and actions, get the process moving.
... inspire a shared vision?	• Envision the future • Enlist others	Leaders enable people to join in the direction or vision.
... challenge the process?	• Search for opportunities • Experiment and take risks	Leaders are constantly challenging other people to exceed their own limitations.
... enable others to act?	• Strengthen others • Foster collaboration	Leaders understand that success requires a team effort
... encourage the heart?	• Recognize individual contributions • Celebrate accomplishments	Leaders show regard for the efforts of others and they celebrate team successes.

Meta Programs – are you being filtered out?

On Sunday, we looked at Meta Programs – the mental processes that enable us to filter the mass of information that we take in every day, and decide on which bits to pay attention to. There are two in particular that are particularly relevant to the reviewing progress:

1 Towards – Away From
2 Internal – External.

Remember that those with the Towards preference are going to be focused on the future and what progress has been made towards the agreed goals. Those with the Away From preference will be focused on progress that has enabled the problem to be minimized or reduced. The language and focus used by each preference type is likely to be quite different.

With regard to the internal and external filters, those who are internally referenced will know whether they are doing a good job or not, without having to be told by anyone else. They are therefore likely to work on their tasks independently and you, as their manager, may not get any feedback from them unless you specifically ask for it. This can be unnerving, particularly if you have a need to know how things are progressing or you don't entirely trust your team members.

Those who have an external filter are probably going to be seeking your approval at more regular intervals, and this can have its disadvantages, particularly if they lack confidence. It can often mean that a manager ends up doing most of the work themselves, rather than investing their time in supporting and building the confidence of the team member to trust their own capabilities.

So, rather than taking a job back to do it yourself, it can be more beneficial in the long term if you ask the person to come prepared with possible solutions rather than bringing problems for you to solve. You can then ask questions to encourage them to think, rather than telling them what to do, which reduces their autonomy and therefore their sense of personal satisfaction in completing the work. It's also important to provide recognition (e.g. 'I believe you have the capability to do this') so that they know you are supporting them.

Here are some questions to use:

- 'What is it that you want to achieve?'
- 'What alternatives do you suggest?'
- 'What are the pros and cons of each idea?'
- 'If you were in charge, which option would you select, and why?'
- 'What might happen if we don't...?'
- 'What else do you think is possible?'

Monitoring tools

As a manager or leader, knowing how things are progressing is important. However, sometimes the process of monitoring can be demotivating to a greater or lesser extent for those who are doing the task being monitored. Therefore, how you have agreed

- what is being measured
- for what purpose *it is being measured*
- what the information is used for

will have a significant bearing on people's motivation to do the task.

It is important that the tool you select is right for the individual and not biased by your own preferences. An effective method for trying to find the appropriate balance between retaining control and delegating is to ask the person who is carrying out the task to write down all the decisions that they regularly have to handle in performing their function. This can be done just by asking them to make a list or by being more creative and brainstorming the question to see whether you can flush out some of the other, more unusual functions and decisions they have to handle. In some cases, it may be preferable for the manager to generate and maintain the list themselves.

The RADAR system below offers a useful way to ensure that everyone is clear about what activities are being monitored, and how.

The RADAR system

Job/task	Recommend	Act	Delegate	Alerts	Reviews
A				Face to face	Daily
B				Email/phone	Weekly – Thursday
C				Email report	Weekly – Monday 1hr (phone) Monthly – 2 hrs (face-to-face meeting)

Together with your team member, use this table to outline the list of jobs or tasks, and agree in which one of the three columns (Recommend, Act, Delegate) the task should be placed.

- **Recommend** This means that when the decision occurs the person comes directly to you with a recommended course of action, and will take no further action without your agreement.
- **Act** This indicates that the person can make the decision themselves.
- **Delegate** This indicates that the person will be delegating the decision to someone who reports to them (i.e. the decision need no longer appear on their list).

Depending on the nature of the job and the relationship you have with the team member, you may also want to discuss and agree the way in which you wish to be informed of alerts or issues. These two final columns, 'Alerts' and 'Reviews', are where you state how often you will review the task and also the communication style of that review (e.g. face-to-face meeting, telephone/Skype call, email report).

- **Alert** This confirms the way in which you would like to be informed of issues or alerts.
- **Review** This describes the type of review (e.g., frequency, type, location) and, perhaps, those attending.

Once you have generated this list, it can be advantageous to consolidate it into a series of subject headings and/or themes.

Review using Action-Centred Leadership

Case study: the high cost of completing a task

These days, the activity of reviewing is probably carried out less often than it ought to be because, often, once a task has been completed, people move straight on to the next activity without reflecting on what has happened during the previous one.

Milo's team had worked really hard to deliver the software upgrade on time, but it had been achieved at the cost of team cohesion. If Milo had asked the team members whether they wanted to work together on another project in future, the answer would have been a resounding 'no'. This was because Milo has encouraged the team to focus solely on the completion of the task, and ignored the team and individual functions.

If, however, Milo had invested some time in maintaining morale, attending to personal problems and giving praise and feedback, he could have helped to create a high-performing team with a strong sense of identity and belonging.

If you are a manager, you need to make sure that you use mechanisms to review progress regarding not just the task but also team and individual functions. That can be as simple as asking the team to score themselves on their team effectiveness on a scale of 1 to 10, and then, if this is low, asking them what needs to change in order to make the score increase. You can use the checklist below as a way of ensuring that you have paid attention to all three areas – task, team and individual. This is based on the Action-Centred Leadership model described on Wednesday.

SUNDAY
MONDAY
TUESDAY
WEDNESDAY
THURSDAY
FRIDAY
SATURDAY

Task, team and Individual functions checklist

Task functions – sense of direction	Tick [✓]	Team functions – sense of belonging	Tick [✓]	Individual functions – sense of identity	Tick [✓]
Achieving objectives		Maintaining morale – building team spirit		Meeting the needs of individuals (within the group)	
Defining group tasks		Cohesiveness of the group		Attending to personal problems	
Planning the work		Setting standards and maintaining discipline		Giving praise and feedback (performance and progress)	
Allocation of resource		Systems for communication		Resolving conflicts	
Organization of duties and responsibilities		Training – the team		Training	
Controlling quality		Selection of sub-leaders		One-to-one meetings	
Monitoring performance					
Reviewing progress					
Achieving objectives					

Summary

Today you have discovered how reviewing progress is a motivational tool in itself, though its effectiveness depends, of course, on how it is used. Reviewing can provide the 'motive for action' and helps individuals to pay attention to what they can proactively do, rather than being passive and waiting for others to take action.

Now that you have spent a week reading about motivating others, you should consider how you are going to put this all into practice. Remember that in order to motivate others you must begin by motivating yourself. When you find that energy and enthusiasm it will rub off on others, and you will be able to start off your actions on a positive note. If the going gets tough, there are many tools in this book that can help you to overcome challenges and deliver results by motivating your team.

So get started now, and see what amazing things you can influence others to achieve.

SUNDAY

MONDAY

TUESDAY

WEDNESDAY

THURSDAY

FRIDAY

SATURDAY

Fact-check [answers at the back]

1. Measurement is a key part of the process of motivation because:
   a) It also begins with the letter 'M' ❏
   b) The activity of measuring progress can provide the ongoing 'motive for action' ❏
   c) It is like an incentive ❏
   d) It gives you extrinsic motivation ❏

2. Before you begin the process of reviewing someone else's performance, you should:
   a) Be clear about how your own performance may have influenced it ❏
   b) Prepare a plan ❏
   c) Observe them to get your own perspective ❏
   d) Be prepared to shout at them if they have not delivered results ❏

3. What type of questions help people to assess their intrinsic motivation?
   a) Open questions ❏
   b) Hypothetical questions ❏
   c) Leading questions ❏
   d) Active questions ❏

4. If a person is given a task to deliver and another department does not provide the information, what generation of employee is likely to be proactive and seek alternative ways to find the solution?
   a) Millennials ❏
   b) Generation X ❏
   c) Traditionalists ❏
   d) Baby boomers ❏

5. According to Kouzes and Posner, which of the following is *not* a characteristic of exemplary leadership?
   a) Challenging the process ❏
   b) Inspiring a shared vision ❏
   c) Enabling others to act ❏
   d) Rearranging priorities ❏

6. Those who are 'internally referenced' are likely to update you on progress:
   a) Rarely, unless you have agreed it with them ❏
   b) Daily ❏
   c) Weekly ❏
   d) At team meetings ❏

7. The D in the RADAR monitoring tool stands for:
   a) Drive ❏
   b) Delegate ❏
   c) Defer until later ❏
   d) Daily monitoring ❏

8. Which of the following is *not* one of the senses to be measured in the Action-Centred Leadership model?
a) Sense of direction ❏
b) Sense of belonging ❏
c) Sense of identify ❏
d) Sense of motivation ❏

9. The Law of Reciprocity is based on the idea that:
a) Feedback drives the motive for action ❏
b) People who are extrinsically motivated will be satisfied only in the short term ❏
c) What you put out you get back ❏
d) 80 per cent of motivational issues are caused by 20 per cent of your people ❏

10. Measuring progress should be carried out:
a) Rarely, because it takes too much time ❏
b) As a part of the process of setting and achieving goals ❏
c) Only by the person doing the job ❏
d) Only if it provide quantitative results ❏

Surviving in tough times

It can be tough to motivate other people in times of change and uncertainty, because their focus tends to go inward and can be driven by fears about financial security or future job prospects. It is therefore down to you to set the tone and, through your actions, provide inspiration and encouragement. By addressing the tips below you can motivate other people to achieve more than they thought possible.

1 You need to be motivated

In order to motivate others you must first be motivated yourself. Reconnect with what makes you feel excited and energized at work – your own motivation needs to come from within you. Once you find your own spark and enthusiasm, it can rub off on others, so start with *you*!

2 Understand the bigger picture

At work, most people these days operate as part of a larger system. That could be their department, division, region, group or country. And, of course, the extra-organizational environment (e.g. the prevailing economic conditions) will have an important impact, too. To motivate people effectively, you should try to understand the bigger picture, and the factors that may be influencing the situation outside your immediate focus.

3 Understand what drives behaviour

People behave in different ways at work in order to satisfy their underlying needs. Whether this is the need for achievement, esteem, belonging, security, power and so on, it is your job as manager to know what these needs are and what is driving them.

4 Create the right environment

The environment in which you work is a key influence on your level of motivation. So, if you want to motivate others, give consideration to their physical working conditions, rewards, interpersonal relations, and the support they get. By creating an environment where people have targets that are realistic yet challenging, and have an opportunity to collaborate and get recognition, you will make a positive impact.

5 Be a role model

Providing inspiration as a manager or leader is not just an add-on to your job; it is an essential element. What you do will be noticed by other people, so it is vital that you 'walk the talk' and act in accordance with the organization's values and behaviours. If you are prepared to do what needs to be done, others are more likely to be prepared to do the same.

6 Consider how, when and why you communicate

Develop an understanding of the subtleties of communication. Whether it is non-verbal behaviour, the language that others use, or what is not said, the way to build rapport and trust with others is to communicate effectively. The greater flexibility you have in your communication style, the easier it will be to influence other people.

7 Make the personal connection

No matter how busy you are, take time to speak to your team face to face and really listen to what they have to say. They will notice that you have made the effort and it will enable you to develop a better relationship with them. If you work remotely, make a phone call or have a video conference, and show that you value them as *individuals*.

8 Provide a level of autonomy

By enabling other people to have a level of control and choice over what they do, you will help them to meet their needs for autonomy, competence and relatedness. This means that individuals will show more creativity, improve their task performance and be in a more positive emotional state. So, even if a job seems clearly defined, find a way to introduce an element of self-determination.

9 Treat each person as an individual

No two people are the same, and therefore a 'one size fits all' approach is of limited use to you as a manager. Take time to get to know each person you have to motivate, and work out what makes them tick. Connecting with them as human beings is far more effective than leaving them feeling they are 'just another number' in the team.

10 Provide recognition and appreciation

It costs nothing to say 'Thank you' or 'Well done' and it can make a huge difference to others. Make sure you that can catch people when they do something right and tell them what you noticed. Work on the principle of giving credit to others, no matter how small their contribution.

References and further reading

Adair, J.E., *Action-Centered Leadership* (New York: McGraw-Hill, 1973).

——, *The John Adair Handbook of Management and Leadership* (London: Thorogood, 2004).

Cohen, A.R., and D.L. Bradford, *Influence without Authority, 2nd edn* (Hoboken, NJ: John Wiley, 2005).

Drucker, P., *Innovation and Entrepreneurship* (New York: Harper & Row, 1985).

Goldsmith, M., *Mojo: How to Get it, How to Keep It and How to Get It Back If You Lose It* (New York: Hyperion, 2010).

Herzberg, F., B. Mausner and B.B. Snyderman, 2nd edn, *The Motivation to Work* (New York: John Wiley, 1959).

Kahneman, D., and A. Tversky, 'Choices, Values, and Frames', *American Psychologist 39*:4 (1984): 341–50.

Kouzes, J. and B. Posner, *The Leadership Challenge: How to Make Extraordinary Things Happen in Organizations*, 4th edn (Hoboken, NJ: Jossey-Bass, 2012).

McGregor, D., *The Human Side of Enterprise* (New York: McGraw-Hill, 1960).

Pink, D.H., *Drive: The Surprising Truth about What Motivates Us* (Edinburgh: Canongate Books, 2009).

Ryan, R.M., and E.L. Deci, 'Self-determination Theory and the Facilitation of Intrinsic Motivation, Social Development, and Well-being', *American Psychologist* 55 (2000), 68–78.

——, 'The "What" and "Why" of Goal Pursuits: Human Needs and the Self-determination of Behaviour', *Psychological Inquiry* 11 (2000), 227–68.

Tannenbaum, R., and W.H. Schmidt, 'How to Choose a Leadership Pattern', *Harvard Business Review* 36 (March–April), 95–101.

Zenger, J., J. Folkman and S. Edinger, *The Inspiring Leader* (New York: McGraw-Hill, 2009).

Zingheim, P.K., and J.R. Schuster, *Pay People Right!* (New York: Jossey-Bass, 2000).

Answers

Sunday: 1b; 2a; 3d; 4c; 5b; 6c; 7d; 8a; 9b; 10a·

Monday: 1a; 2c; 3d; 4a; 5a; 6b; 7b; 8d; 9a; 10b

Tuesday: 1a; 2d; 3c; 4c; 5c; 6a; 7d; 8d; 9b; 10b

Wednesday: 1b; 2d; 3a; 4c; 5d; 6d; 7a; 8b; 9a; 10c

Thursday: 1b; 2c; 3c; 4a; 5d; 6c; 7d; 8a; 9a; 10b & c

Friday: 1d; 2a; 3b; 4d; 5a; 6a; 7c; 8d; 9b; 10d

Saturday: 1b; 2a; 3d; 4b; 5d; 6a; 7b; 8d; 9c; 10b